D1601397

FROM THE FIELD
TO THE
LEGISLATURE

Recent Titles in
Contributions in Women's Studies

White Women Writing White: H.D., Elizabeth Bishop, Sylvia Plath, and Whiteness
Renée R. Curry

The Foreign Woman in British Literature: Exotics, Aliens, and Outsiders
Marilyn Demarest Button and Toni Reed, editors

Embracing Space: Spatial Metaphors in Feminist Discourse
Kerstin W. Shands

On Top of the World: Women's Political Leadership in Scandinavia and Beyond
Bruce O. Solheim

Victorian London's Middle-Class Housewife: What She Did All Day
Yaffa Claire Draznin

Connecting Links: The British and American Woman Suffrage Movements, 1900–1914
Patricia Greenwood Harrison

Female Journeys: Autobiographical Expressions by French and Italian Women
Claire Marrone

Excluded from Suffrage History: Matilda Joslyn Gage, Nineteenth-Century American Feminist
Leila R. Brammer

The Artist as Outsider in the Novels of Toni Morrison and Virginia Woolf
Lisa Williams

(Out)Classed Women: Contemporary Chicana Writers on Inequitable Gendered Power Relations
Phillipa Kafka

"Saddling La Gringa": Gatekeeping in Literature by Contemporary Latina Writers
Phillipa Kafka

Representing the Marginal Woman in Nineteenth-Century Russian Literature: Personalism, Feminism, and Polyphony
Svetlana Slavskaya Grenier

FROM THE FIELD TO THE LEGISLATURE

A History of Women in the Virgin Islands

Eugenia O'Neal

Contributions in Women's Studies, Number 187

GREENWOOD PRESS
Westport, Connecticut • London

Library of Congress Cataloging-in-Publication Data

O'Neal, Eugenia, 1965–
    From the field to the legislature : a history of women in the Virgin Islands /
Eugenia O'Neal.
       p. cm.—(Contributions in women's studies, ISSN 0147–104X ; no. 187)
    Includes bibliographical references and index.
    ISBN 0–313–31756–9 (alk. paper)
    1. Women—British Virgin Islands—History. I. Title. II. Series.
HQ1525.4.O53 2001
305.4'097297'25—dc21   00–057810

British Library Cataloguing in Publication Data is available.

Library of Congress Catalog Card Number: 00–057810
ISBN: 0–313–31756–9
ISSN: 0147–104X

First published in 2001

Greenwood Press, 88 Post Road West, Westport, CT 06881
An imprint of Greenwood Publishing Group, Inc.
www.greenwood.com

Printed in the United States of America

The paper used in this book complies with the
Permanent Paper Standard issued by the National
Information Standards Organization (Z39.48–1984).

10 9 8 7 6 5 4 3 2 1

Copyright Acknowledgment

The author and publisher gratefully acknowledge permission for use of the following material:

Selected material from the author's inteview with Eileene Parsons, 12 August 1998, Road
Town. Reprinted by permission of Ms. Parsons.

This work is dedicated to the memory of
Antonia Jimenez de O'Neal and Gertrude O'Neal

Contents

Preface

Colonialism, at least in its most overt form, is largely extinct in much of the world. A relic of a bygone era, it has been shelved among the mothballs of history. Not so in the Virgin Islands, a tiny outpost of the empire on which the sun famously never set. Like the other United Kingdom Overseas Territories in the Caribbean, the Virgin Islands has been content, despite gentle prodding from the United Nations De-Colonization Committee, to remain a colony.

Yet the Virgin Islands has, in the last couple of decades, carved out a fairly autonomous role for itself in the region and the world. Left to its own devices after the abolition of slavery, the territory saw to its own economic survival, asking nothing from Britain and, indeed, receiving next to nothing. Then came industrialization and air travel and disposable income. Before long, the territory had developed a thriving tourism industry. The Virgin Islands, a colony but an increasingly rich one, became a magnet for migrants from the other, recently independent Caribbean islands. Then came high taxes in rich countries and clever lawyers and almost overnight the financial services sector was the "twin pillar" of the Virgin Islands economy. The United Kingdom pinched itself and began to take an interest in the colony's affairs. Drug use was a big issue in the metropolitan countries, so drug trafficking became a big issue in these islands, which once touted themselves as "Nature's Little Secrets." The colonial relationship changed and reshaped itself.

De Beauvoir could have said not only that "one is not born, but rather becomes a woman" but that one also becomes colonized. The relation between patriarchal stereotypes of womanhood and colonial stereotypes of the colonized are clear: Both woman and the colonized are in need of a firm hand and guidance. Just as woman is considered by patriarchy to be inferior to man, valuable in her obedience and subservience, so also is the colonized thought to be inferior to the colonizer. How, then, have these twin jeopardies interacted to influence and shape the lives of Virgin Islands women? How have women perceived their personal and professional obligations in a sociopolitical order structured by patriarchy and colonialism? Since women have been invisible in much of the scholarship on the Virgin Islands, finding the answer to these questions has been difficult and, it could be argued, still incomplete. Women's names appear on school buildings, but they do not appear in the textbooks read inside.

As a woman born in not just a colonial society but in the colonial society of the Virgin Islands I wanted to explore how women have defined and are defining themselves in relation to their society.

Even as the colonial relationship is redefining itself in the face of modern pressures, so are Virgin Islands women redefining themselves and their role in their society. I wanted to show the ways they have done that ever since their arrival in this part of the world. I hope that dedicating an entire book to them, to their achievements, and also to their failings will serve not only as an acknowledgment of their presence in, and importance to, the fabric of Virgin Islands society, but also as a signpost for further research into women's lives in these islands.

This work could never have been written without the assistance and support of various individuals and organizations. I am indebted to Dr. Eudine Barriteau and Dr. George Belle of the University of the West Indies, who were responsible for supervising the research on which this book is based. Staffers at the Public Record Office; the National Archives in the United Kingdom, Barbados, and the Road Town Public Library in Tortola were always courteous and helpful. Without the assistance of the Training Division of the Government of the Virgin Islands and the British Development Division, I would never have been able to undertake this work, so I am very grateful to them. I would also like to acknowledge with affection the support and assistance of my friends, in particular, Linnell Abbott, Elise Donovan, Sandra D. Crawford, Kathy Smith, Dora Harrigan, and Diane Solomon.

Introduction

Although several books and studies have concerned themselves with the history of these islands, none has made women its focus. Further, those books that have been written about Caribbean women have not offered any consideration of Virgin Islands women. And none has explored the impact of evolving colonial policies on women's status within a society that remains colonized in the twenty-first century. This book is an effort to recognize and restore women to their rightful place as equal contributors to Virgin Islands society. It explores the extent to which, despite the patriarchal context in which colonialism originated, Virgin Islands women created opportunities that ensured their economic survival and assured them of leadership positions within their communities.

During slavery, planters manipulated gender ideology to argue that black women were more like men and not at all like the women of Europe. In negating the humanity of black people, planters denied any relationship between black women and traditional European ideas of femininity. Gender ideologies were massaged in the employ of planters' economic purposes. Not until the abolition movement made significant headway in the British Parliament did planters begin to make concessions for enslaved black women that were in keeping with patriarchal ideas about women's weaknesses. Established and created by European men, steeped in notions of male superiority and female inferiority, colonial plantation society was the backdrop against which competing interests warred for the right to define black womanhood. Ideas on black women and black womanhood resembled a shifting canvas to which more and more values associated with white womanhood were added until expectations of black women mirrored those of their white counterparts. This book examines that process and looks at the strategies many black Virgin Islands women employed to escape their double colonization and emerge as social, political, and economic leaders.

Virgin Islands women ardently pursued education, perhaps recognizing it as their only avenue of escape from the private sphere and their only means for economic advancement. They established many of the territory's elementary schools and lent their organizational and other skills to the creation of different community services. In doing so, these women created opportunities for themselves, establishing the foundation from which they were to later launch leadership careers in education, the civil service, politics, and business.

This book also comes to terms with the fact that the particular achievements of exceptional Virgin Islands women of the past and present have left untouched the status of the majority of their sisters. Today, women in the Virgin Islands remain concentrated in low-paying, low-status jobs, which has a negative effect on their economic and political power. Though women's church and community groups abound, they have not coalesced into nor inspired a women's movement. In fact, the groups are having the opposite effect. They are segregating women into mutually suspicious factions, proving the assertion that women's isolation from one another is one reason for their failure to constitute a political class or to form a consciousness of themselves as women. It can be argued further that women's participation in church groups is acting to retard their participation in nontraditional areas. The pervasive masculinist reading of the Bible by first the missionaries and subsequently the church leaders (particularly of the fundamentalist sects) may be acting to isolate women from a sense of self as subject. Reddock asserts that participation in religious groups "represents a legitimate space within which women can freely participate outside of the home, without questions or need for justification."[1] But if these groups are isolating women from each other within organizations that are seen as secondary to the management of the church, they are doing more harm than good to women's overall sense of empowerment. In failing to recognize that inequities are not due to personal failure but to a system of discriminatory practices, Virgin Islands women have failed to develop the politicization of group identification.

Virgin Islands men, however, who shared the same masculinist ideology, if not the same race, with the representatives of British imperialism, found and forged a group consciousness and a collective interest in support of their ascendancy to power. They could do this because, as men, their right to political participation was not questioned. Beginning in 1818 when free black men gained the right to elect an assemblyman, it was understood that although race and class might be held against them, their sex posed no obstacle to their involvement in the public sphere. There was no such understanding for women. Having internalized the patriarchal values of the colonizer, women have been unable to forge a group consciousness and a sense of their oppression as women in opposition to male power and dominance (and, by extension, to colonial power). Thus colonialism in the Virgin Islands, while allowing space for men's political participation, could be said to have restricted women's. This book will look at the roles and functions ascribed to and assumed by women and how the colonization process shaped those roles. It will examine how black women, once considered "equal under the whip," have lagged behind men in political achievement.

It will be argued that political power, evolving in a context of continued colonization, has been the property of a small cadre of men. Women's participation in politics has therefore had to contend with a formidable combination of historical and ideological forces arrayed against it.

NOTE

1. Rhoda Reddock, "Women's Organisation in the Caribbean Community from the 19th Century to Today," *Woman Speak*, no. 26 and 27 (December 1990), pp. 17–24.

CHAPTER 1

———•◦◦•———

Slavery

BIRTH OF A COLONY

Columbus stumbled upon what became known as the Virgin Islands during his second voyage in 1493, but the islands were largely ignored by the European powers until the late seventeenth century. They were described by Thomas Coke in the 1800s as mostly consisting of "no other than solitary rocks, presenting to the spectator barren crags, at once destitute of verdure and unfit for cultivation. . . . [The islands] produced no wealth to tempt the invader; and when compared with other Islands, no fertility that could excite allurement, or promise to repay exertion with reward." In short, they seemed of use only to pirates and smugglers hiding out from various European navies. Realizing this potential, Dutch buccaneers built a fort on Tortola in 1648. They managed to hold on to it for eighteen years until they were finally routed by the English. From then on, Tortola, Jost Van Dyke, Virgin Gorda, Guana, Beef, Thatch, Anegada, and several other smaller islands belonged to the British, whereas the remaining islands were split between the Danes and the Spanish. In 1672, through a grant by Charles II, the islands were put under the administration of the government of the Leeward Islands, headquartered in Antigua.

Government supervision of the tiny and far-flung islands was intermittent and slight. Several efforts at colonization were abandoned in the face of attacks by the Spanish and by pirates from various European countries. Defeated by the mountainous, rocky terrain and in the absence of any local government administration, some settlers turned to smuggling themselves.

In 1724, the governor of the Leeward Islands made an effort to bring the fledgling colony under the rule of law. He appointed a local council of six justices of the peace, a secretary, a provost marshal, and a deputy governor that had legislative and judicial authority. The deputy governor was based at Spanish Town, as the settlement on Virgin Gorda was called. The colony drew settlers from Anguilla, Barbados, and some of the other islands, many of whom brought enslaved Africans with them. But these were not wealthy people. Coke reports that "luxury was a stranger to the island and people bartered among each other."

In 1741, a Fat Hogs Bay planter, John Pickering, was appointed lieutenant governor over the council, which was moved from its seat on Virgin Gorda to Tortola. Virgin Gorda was allowed to keep its deputy governor. From little more than a handful at the turn of the century, the population grew. In 1720, 1,122 whites were recorded as living in the Virgin Islands, as were 1,509 enslaved Africans. Although the number of whites rose slowly, the population of slaves grew quickly. By 1756, there were 1,263 whites and 6,121 blacks.

The deputy governorship in Virgin Gorda was abolished in 1771, and the lieutenant governor in Tortola was given complete authority under the governor of the Leeward Islands, who now made annual visits to the territory. A mere two years later, in 1773, it was conceded that the islands had developed to the point that they were ready to have a two-chambered legislature consisting of twelve members. But only landowners could vote. These restrictions mirrored legislation found in Britain and its other colonies and kept the number of those eligible to vote to a minimum. In this way the planters and the elite of the small colony kept a tight grip on the reins of power. Candidates to the House had to be at least "twenty-one and in possession of 40 pounds sterling or a house worth at least 40 pounds." The governor of the Leeward Islands retained the veto, and the Crown held the power of disallowance. As it is today, the governor continued to hold responsibility for the territory's foreign affairs and for its defense.

The territory prospered and began to acquire those hallmarks that typified the more settled plantation life in much of the rest of the Caribbean. An eighteenth-century observer wrote that "cotton and sugar canes might be seen flourishing on the sides of the mountains; and in the low lands, Ginger was cultivated, and Indigo works appeared."[1] These industries were supported by, and dependent on, the labor of enslaved Africans.

CONSTRUCTING VERSIONS OF WOMANHOOD: PLANTATION SOCIETY, 1700–1834

Slavery was primarily an economic mechanism that came to be founded on racism, an ideology that denied blacks any claim to humanity. Caribbean planters propounded and developed arguments concerning the supposed barbarity and inferiority of blacks. They also denied any claims black women might have made to participate in traditional notions of European femininity. Instead, slave owners allowed themselves access to black women's labor by emphasizing their difference from white women. Caribbean planters were adamant that black women were not like white women. They did not look like them, did not have the perceived delicacy of feature, and in fact, were more like men with wombs. Thus, the planters argued, they deserved no quarter. Like the men they resembled, they were expected to work in the fields and wherever else their owners required them.

The work on plantations was divided in three main ways. The strongest men and women, the first gang, cut the canes, fed the mills, and cleared, holed, and planted the fields. Weeding and lighter work was done by the second gang, which consisted of boys and girls, "women far gone with child," and convalescents. The younger children, shepherded by an elderly woman, made up the third gang, which was responsible for feeding the plantation's livestock.

As in most of the other Caribbean islands, the plantation economy of the Virgin Islands depended heavily on black women's labor. An eighteenth-century Quaker visitor to Tortola recorded his visit to W. R. Isaacs' Pleasant Valley Estate, where he saw "both men and women. . . . busily engaged in preparing the soil for planting. . . . This process of preparing the ground for canes is called 'holeing.' Each labourer has his or her particular portion of duty assigned—some with huge hoes were forming the ridges, others clearing the trench, and others we noticed were carrying stones upon their heads to make embankments."[2]

Preparing the ground, or holeing, was said by many contemporary observers to be the hardest work on the plantation. In the Virgin Islands it would have been particularly hard given the stony, rocky nature of the soil, but black women were not excused from this or any other aspect of field work. At Tortola's Mount Healthy, another visitor observed "about fifty or sixty men and women employed cutting the sugar canes on an inclined plane near the summit and in shooting them down the troughs."[3]

Enslaved women also worked as drivers, a position that in many other Caribbean islands was reserved for slave men.[4] A woman complains in an 1824 report on slave conditions in the Virgin Islands that "the driver woman, Emmy, sometimes licked her with a small broom brush."[5]

On a small island, population concerns may have driven planters to exploit black women's labor in whatever ways they could. Had planters observed a division of labor in the status position of driver, the slave-to-white ratio might have been even greater and therefore more troubling. By the 1820s, the ratio stood at almost eight slaves to one white.

The fact that plantations in the Virgin Islands were, on average, smaller than those in the bigger countries would also have affected planters' capacity to restrict labor by sex. The ratio of enslaved men to enslaved women in the territory was approximately 86:100.[6] In 1825, there were 2,506 enslaved males compared with 2,942 females, and in 1828, there were 2,498 enslaved males and 2,894 females. Though plantation records for the territory are rare, it is notable that the adult females freed by the Nottingham family outnumbered the adult males almost two to one.[7] Black women provided the estates with a significant percentage of slave labor, and they did so at a cheaper cost than black men. Certainly, plantations in the Virgin Islands were generally poorer than those in the larger Caribbean islands; planters may simply not have been able to afford the higher prices charged for enslaved males. In any case, the territory was often the last stop for slavers coming up the island chain from Barbados. Estate owners on the other islands would have had the first pick of the enslaved people on board.

In addition to field work, black women performed duties that were more in keeping with both European and African traditional expectations of women. Many worked as washers, cooks, house servants, seamstresses, and laundresses within the estates and in the larger society. A visitor to Tortola in the 1820s described encountering "five or six negro women, who had been engaged in washing clothes in the shallow stream which meandered through the irregular courses of the ravine."

For black women, balancing their slave lives with family responsibilities must have been a difficult challenge. Their additional responsibilities included cleaning their own homes, washing the family laundry, child rearing, and cooking for their household. Thomas Moody observed that often "the same female cooked, washed, picked fuel wood and huxtered goods for sale." For them, work in the field, on their grounds, or in the home never stopped. Their lives of hard and constant labor contrasted sharply with the lives of white women.

Poor white women may have been employed in field work at the very beginning of plantation society in the mid-1600s, but by the end of that century, this was no longer the case. A proposal to deport a small group of white convict women from England to Barbados was rebuffed in no uncertain terms. In a 1697 letter to the lords commissioner of trade, the West Indian agent wrote, "It will be no . . . advantage to the island of Barbados to have these women sent thither. For no English women are there put to work in the field." He went on to suggest that "in places where white women work in the field such as Virginia and Carolina, such women as these may be useful and acceptable."[8]

White women, viewed as fragile and angelic, were not expected to work in the field or even to assist in the running of a plantation. The "protection" from the filth and crime of London's streets offered by women's enshrinement in the home was exported to the Caribbean colonies and creolized.

According to Barbadian historian Hillary Beckles, the white woman "was now considered unfit for manual labour on account of her endemic fragility: unsuited to physical exertion in the tropics as a consequence of her possession of a faint heart and delicate skin; terrified of black male sexuality on account of her chaste, virginal and jet-white purity; and devoid of lust, gaiety and passion."[9]

Indeed, Edwards noted that "except for the exercise of dancing... [white women in the Caribbean] have no amusement or avocation to impel them to much exertion of either body or mind." He went on to say that "to a stranger newly arrived, the ladies appear as just risen from the bed of sickness. Their voice is soft and spiritless and every step betrays languor and lassitude." In his *Letters From the Virgin Islands*, Anonymous professed to have been annoyed by white Creole women's "villainous keeping to bed and dormitory." But others were more admiring.

Suckling, in the Virgin Islands in the 1700s, wrote that "few ladies in the West Indies know better how to set out and do the honours of the table than those at Tortola. . . . Their behaviour is polite and their conversation entertaining and sprightly but very delicate and modest. . . . After a proper attention to their family affairs, which are never neglected, their usual amusements are sewing, reading, dancing and sometimes a pool at quadrille."

In creating a society in which the few ruled brutally over the many, white males engineered a society with built-in flaws. Harsh slave codes and punishments are obvious evidence of white men's feelings of insecurity and vulnerability. They could brook no fifth column, no betrayal from their women, the Other who lived in their homes and bore their children, thereby contributing to the perpetuation of their society. To co-opt them, white men placed white women, no matter their social or class origin, on a pedestal. This accomplished two objectives; at one and the same time it ensured white women's collaboration while removing them from the field of battle.

Though they had not created the plantation system, white women contributed to and benefited from the institution of slavery (though perhaps not to the same extent as white men). In 1798, three women—Mrs. Barzey, Mrs. Scatliffe, and Katherine Lake—were listed as owning sizeable plantations on Tortola.[10] Note is also made of a Mrs. Gardiner, whose heirs were in possession of her land.

White women depended heavily on their slaves and owned or supervised many of them. Anonymous wrote of a "Miss Letty, sole white daughter to a justice of the peace," whose father gave her six slaves to take with her upon her marriage. If, as reported by that visitor, "every house swarmed with domestics" (one woman was said to have nineteen) it is little wonder that white women were described as languorous. Even the running of the household, traditionally their domain, was undertaken by others. This investment in slavery meant that many had a lot to lose from slavery's abolition. An 1825 report on the Virgin Islands revealed that when the apprenticeship period of certain Free Africans was up, several white women "were thus thrown upon the parish or poor funds."

Free Africans, or Liberated Africans, as they were also known, had been on slave ships intercepted by the British in or around the Caribbean after 1807. They were taken to the nearest islands and assigned as apprentices to white and free coloreds for an initial period ranging from ten years for men and childless women, to fourteen years for pregnant women. More than a thousand, men, women, and children had been landed on Tortola and apprenticed out in the territory. By 1823, however, there were only 295 apprentices still living in the Virgin Islands. Along with their 88 children, they lived in Kingstown, a special area reserved for them on Tortola. Though the people to whom they were apprenticed were expected to see to their learning a skill and to their moral development, many instead viewed them as another opportunity for profit.

Mrs. Dix, a white woman whose husband had died leaving her in possession of at least twenty liberated Africans, hired them out on St. Thomas. They were said to earn her "a piece of eight of Danish money" or about 2s. 6d. sterling per day. Indeed, after the abolition of the slave trade in 1807, many in poor circumstances, black and white, saw the Free Africans as their last opportunity to obtain free labor and as their ticket to financial solvency. One woman, described as a "female pauper," wanted to obtain "an apprentice from whose labour she thought she could derive great advantage." Everybody wanted to cash in on the labor of blacks, but white women faced a singular disability: the languor and lassitude observed of them in the Caribbean was a function of their idealization as the angels of plantation society. This idealization furthered European men's ends while robbing their women of autonomy and drive. With slaves to direct to every whim, white women were still at a disadvantage—their lives were constrained and restricted by class and by European patriarchal traditions. Under these traditions they could no more go out into the fields or set up shop than black women could become the respected wives of white men.

In his account of the condition of Free Africans in the Virgin Islands, Moody wrote that "the parochial poor are white females and their children in reduced circumstances, from the failure of their husbands or fathers, and generally get support from their relations, otherwise they could not well exist, as there are few modes in which they could exercise their industry, were they more able and inclined to work than they really are."[11] Patriarchy had failed these European women who, unable to depend on the men in their lives, were unable to depend on themselves. Neither able nor inclined to work, they were completely dependent on either the labor of blacks or the beneficence of other whites.

In the 1800s, on Tortola

There lived in a distant part of the island a widow lady, who had been left by a deceased husband with an only daughter, dependent for their subsistence upon the fluctuating and precarious products of the sugar plantation on which they resided. Improvident expenditure had placed the property under mortgage during the proprietor's lifetime, continued depreciation, and bad management had reduced the surplus income to a portion scarce sufficient to support his widow and child.[12]

These women were living the dark flip side of the patriarchal myths that both enshrined and imprisoned them in the home. The loss of a breadwinner who had not provided for his dependents in the event of his death left white women vulnerable to challenges few knew how to face and surmount.

In contrast, slave owners' refusal to allow black women to share notions of European femininity functioned to absolve them of blame for black women's status and condition. Pregnant black women could continue to be worked in the fields given their "Amazon" nature, but white women were expected to "lie in" for the duration of their confinement. Following birth white women stayed at home, often in bed, for weeks and months. The slave woman, on the other hand, was given little or no time following birth to care and nurture her child. Economic imperatives required her quick return to the fields, so plantation society attributed to the black woman those qualities that allowed the almost uninterrupted exploitation of both her labor and her reproductive capacity. Black women were therefore described as having very little of the maternal feeling with which white women were imbued.[13] Required to be at her master's sexual beck and call, the black woman was represented as promiscuous, immoral, unchaste, and a bad mother. It did not help that plantation owners and managers cared little about properly clothing their slave women. Anonymous, commenting on conditions on estates in the Virgin Islands, noted that many visitors to the West Indies "express disgust at the want of decency in attire so rife among the praedial slaves, more especially the females here. . . . For the more elderly and those whose naked imps bestride [their hips] the decencies of clothing are kept only in name." As Bush argues, black women's nakedness contributed to their being stereotyped as bad and immoral women.

Edwards wrote that "they hold chastity in so little estimation that barrenness and frequent abortions, the usual effects of a promiscuous intercourse, are very generally prevalent among them. To the same origin may be ascribed that neglect and want of maternal affection towards the children . . . observable in many of the Black females."[14] By contrast, he noted that white Creole women's "native goodness of heart and gentleness of disposition [combined] with their system of life and manners (sequestered, domestic and unobtrusive)" contributed to the fact that "no women on earth make better wives, or better mothers."

Derogatory observations of black women were meant to create and sustain a perception of their inferiority to white women. Everything that white women were—maternal, modest, and virtuous—was said to be everything that black women were not. But in providing the dominant agricultural labor input on the estates, black women assumed a sense of themselves as agents that allowed them to forge leadership roles within the black community. Freed from the limited and limiting expectations of European-style femininity, many led lives of relative economic and sexual freedom while contributing to the well-being of their families and communities.

FINDING FREEDOM AND RESISTING DEFINITION

Black women in the Virgin Islands subverted or resisted slavery in direct and indirect ways. Resistance quite often took the form of running away, some going as far as Puerto Rico, a much bigger island in whose forests runaways could lose themselves. The "Return of the nature and number of punishments inflicted by the authority of the Stipendiary Magistrate" from 1 September 1834 to 1 August 1835 indicates that twenty-two of the forty-seven apprentices punished for running away were women. Black women's sex clearly was no impediment in their resistance to enslavement. According to this return, women were also punished for theft, disobedience of orders, destruction of property (which included the breaking of canes), neglect of duty, resistance to commands, and absenteeism. The story of one woman, Mary, apprenticed to Dr. Porter, president of the territory, demonstrates how strongly some free African women balked at their virtual enslavement as apprentices. Porter, complaining about Mary's indolence and neglect of duty, confined her (we are not told where but it may have been the jail); when that did not succeed in making her a more satisfactory worker, he took her before the magistrates. They refused to interfere, so Porter ended by whipping her.

Black women's sex did not make any difference in their punishment. Black men and women found guilty of offenses against the plantation system were subject to whipping with confinement and hard labor. Only during amelioration did this change; women were still subject to confinement with hard labor, but whipping them was forbidden. By the early 1830s, hard labor meant cleaning the church and prison yard while working in irons from eight in the morning until four in the afternoon. Laborers who did not work in the yard were often sent to work on estates.

Another form of resistance employed by slave women was self-mutilation. George Porter reported that, in 1793, a pact was made among some of the slaves on Tortola. Each would cut off "his or her left arm so as to disable them from future work." He goes on to recount that "in the space of one month, eight Negroes, two of which were women had their Bills ground sharp and deliberately performed this operation on themselves."

Porter saw this as evidence of wildness and heathenism, and it is no coincidence that it occurred among field slaves. They were not only the ones worked the hardest on the plantation, they were also the ones who had the least contact with white society. Moreover, Tortola planters relied heavily on the purchase of enslaved African peoples rather than on "natural increase."[15] Field workers, fresh from Africa and living at a greater remove from white society, evinced a stronger attachment and reverence for African cultural norms and practices than their domestic counterparts. A Methodist missionary in the Virgin Islands writing in the early 1800s said that field negroes "believe in the existence of spirits, which they call Jumbees and sometimes spread victuals on the graves of those who were recently dead, that their spirits might return and eat."[16] It was also reported that the territory's "negroes and more particularly those brought from Africa wear amulets composed of any and every thing according to their own caprice."[17] These observations bear out the contention that field slaves "remained the most isolated and the most 'African' group" in Caribbean society. Since "everything African was held to be, by definition, inferior" resistance for the field slaves was found in holding on to past traditions and practices in whatever manner possible. Preserving these connections with their past not only strengthened slaves' ability to retain a sense of personhood but also helped to secure new community ties. In spreading food on the graves, for instance, Africans demonstrated their respect for those who had passed on. Perhaps even more importantly, they also claimed their role in a tradition that recognized an individual's connection to all who had gone before and, implicitly, all who were to come. In doing so, they anchored themselves in their community in a way that Porter could not have understood.

Besides these subtle and not so subtle methods, there were the uprisings. Jamaican sociologist Orlando Patterson gives several reasons for slave revolts in the Caribbean, including a high ratio of slaves to whites, a high ratio of African slaves to Creoles, the geography of the islands, a high degree of absenteeism, and the impact of social, religious, and political forces on the slaves. These factors were all present to one degree or another in the Virgin Islands. By 1810, for instance, the governor of the Leeward Islands was already complaining that many of the proprietors on the smaller islands no longer lived on their estates and that only a "few white inhabitants" remained. The geography of the many scattered islands provided unique opportunities for running away from one island to the next and escaping punishment, as has already been discussed. And abolitionist agitation may bear the greatest responsibility for the fact that in the 1820s when abolitionists were extremely active, there were four rebellions in the Virgin Islands.

Patterson describes the three types of slave rebellions. The first was spontaneous, hastily conceived, and restricted to one plantation or small area. The second was planned and was meant to involve all slaves and to overthrow the rule of the whites. The last type involved enslaved people who had run away. Of the six known slave rebellions in the Virgin Islands, all except the last in 1831 were in the first category.

Other ways of attempting to escape the slave system were much more subtle. For some enslaved women, finding a white protector was seen as a chance at freedom and providing a better life for themselves and their children. They therefore manipulated their femininity to become more attractive to white men. An eighteenth-century author noted that female slaves in constant contact with whites, such as the light-skinned housekeepers and long-term mistresses of white men, modeled their conduct on that of white women.[18] The racial ideology of the time determined that both the tar brush and the whitewash should map out individual destiny. If, as many whites argued, one lick with the tar brush immediately painted one black, then many took it as a necessary corollary that a discernible infusion of white ancestry should privilege those considered lucky enough to have it. Thus, the lighter the women (and men) were, the further the field retreated for them and for their mulatto children.[19] By adopting the customs and behavior of white women, enslaved women demonstrated the artificiality of racial and gender stereotypes while providing a subtle resistance to common representations of them.

Mulatto women were particularly admired and sought after by white men. Anonymous noted that "the notice of strangers in this climate will be much drawn to the free women of colour, most of whom—as is generally known—live par amours with white men." Even John Coakley Lettsom, a Quaker and a leading luminary of the London medical scene who founded the Royal Medical Society, was not immune. After an absence of more than twenty years from the country of his birth, Lettsom returned to the Virgin Islands in 1768 for a period of six months. He bought a woman while there whom he described in admiring terms. Teresa was, he said, "a beautiful mulatto of mine. She has long hair, is a brunette, but has such a pleasing and fine eye, and such symmetry of shape, that many West Indians would have placed her on the head of a black seraglio."[20]

Lettsom bought Teresa and another slave, Sam, from his stepfather for £200, but despite her beauty, he did not take her back with him and Sam to England, and we know little else about her. Presumably Teresa earned her keep through her own industry and initiative, living a fairly independent life until Lettsom freed her in 1782.

Evidence exists of the benefits some black women received from their liaisons with white men. According to an 1825 Virgin Islands report, "William Johnston, a mariner, a white man, purchased [Mary, a mulatto], also his two children by her; they live with him and keep his house." Though sexual encounters between white men and black women were not, of course, all consensual, the above case demonstrates evidence of a long-standing relationship. That Mary bore William's children while enslaved to another owner also suggests some freedom of choice on her part.

Kitty, an enslaved woman freed along with nineteen others by their owner Mirriam Harragin, was reported in 1824 to be living with "Benjamin

Penn of Great Camanoes, a white man and cotton planter since her freedom and has had four more mulatto children. . . . Seven of her children are entirely supported by Mr. Penn. None of them cultivate any ground."[21] Examples like these abound. Moody reported that a free colored woman was the kept mistress of Mr. McInrot, Dougan's clerk when he was the navy agent in Tortola.

White men's marriages to white women proved no obstacle to these liaisons. Mark Dyer French, married and "with an amiable family," had an outside relationship with a woman named Anne, whom he manumitted.

Although it could be said that Kitty and Mary and others like them bought into a patriarchal definition of womanhood, their ability to do so in the context of a society that denied them their very humanity was nevertheless an achievement. Denigrated as promiscuous, some black women yearned for the respectability and security white women enjoyed. They used their relationships with men, black and white, to create this respectability and security for themselves. Beckles says "it was commonly agreed that prominent white men should not marry [mulatto women] or allow them to transcend white women in social respectability." And the reports above do seem to prove that point, since they do not say the couples were married. However, these liaisons between black women and white men *did* improve the women's status, if only within the black community. If of a long-standing duration as with Mary and Kitty, the relationships also served as a hands-off signal to other white men in a time when there was a sexual open season on black women's bodies.[22]

For some women, their liaisons with white men resulted not only in freedom for themselves and their children but also in the acquisition of property. One of the most prosperous slave owners in the Virgin Islands, George Martin, left a will directing that his property be divided among the children he had fathered by several slave women. All of them, along with their mothers, were manumitted by his will. At the time of his death, he owned 720 slaves, two houses, two sloops, and five sugar estates. He also bequeathed six slaves to one mulatto woman, Bice, who was said to be his favorite.

These relationships between white men and black women should not be taken to mean that the latter had it any easier under slavery than black men. In his report on the Free Africans, Moody pointed out that "the greatest number of cases of maltreatment, which came before us, related to females . . . it nowhere appears that they were better treated than the males."

Arthur Hodge, who was later hanged for the murder of Prosper, a male slave, killed both male and female slaves through the severity of his punishments.

Having suspected two female slaves, Margaret, his cook, and Else, a washerwoman, of a design to poison Mrs. Hodge and his children, he poured a quantity of boiling water down their throats; and having after this severely cart-whipped them and chained them together, he sent them, in a state of entire nakedness, to work in the field. Both these slaves languished for a short time in a miserable condition and then died. On the day that Margaret died, one of the deponents going into the kitchen, and observing she was stupefied, asked her what was the matter; on which she pulled a handkerchief from her head, and shewed [sic] two very severe wounds, which she said Mr. Hodge had given her. She soon after fell on her face, and, being carried to the sick-house, died that evening.[23]

In another instance noted in the depositions taken before his trial, Hodge had an enslaved woman named Violet "confined and severely flogged and cut by him, for the alleged crime of stealing candles."

Children were not immune to Hodge's cruelties either. "A Mulatto child reputed to be his own, named Bella, was repeatedly cart-whipped, by his order; and he was also seen repeatedly to strike the child with a stick on the head, so as to break her head; and also to kick her so violently as to send her several feet on the ground."

These examples serve to illustrate the harsh realities of slavery. Black women were no less subject to these by reason of their gender.

Besides outright cruelty, black women, like black men, were also subject to simple neglect. Of the 51 women manumitted between 1818 and 1822, eleven were between sixty-three and eighty-nine years and incapable of hard agricultural labor. These women had become superfluous to the purpose of the estates—profit. Unable to exploit either their bodies or their labor, plantation owners had no further use for aged black women. One observer acknowledged that "it is by no means unusual for slaves of little value to hold the enviable privilege of shifting for themselves." This "enviable privilege" meant that many, like the woman Dorcas whom the writer himself mentions, were reduced to begging for charity.

In the face of both the petty and violent cruelties of plantation life, black men and women relied on each other for support and strength. Bush argues that the "family tree was not cut" by enslavement but that loving relationships between men and women existed. These relationships were, however, threatened by sale and removal. Removals to other islands or countries were common throughout the colony's history. In 1799, Coke reported "great numbers" of removals to Demerara while, in 1803, 259 slaves were taken away from the territory. Decades later, in 1823, it was reported that because of the "poverty of a great part of the land . . . a great many Negroes [from Road Town and East End] were taken away." Some may have accepted this disruption to their family ties, but others did not. Coke recounts the story of Isaac Vanterpool, who was sold away from his wife and child on Virgin Gorda to a planter on Tortola. Two years later he was resold to someone on St. Eustatius, many miles from Virgin Gorda. Vanterpool ran away, catching a boat back to his family in the Virgin Islands. Captured and sent back to St. Eustatius, he must have convinced his owner that he would run away again, because he was soon resold to a Virgin Gordian. That story had a relatively happy ending, but many others did not.

Some black women found both love and freedom through their relationships with black men. In one instance, "William Nibbs, a carpenter and free man of colour . . . purchased this woman and three children, . . . he manumitted them and now supports them by his industry, aided by that of the mother," who worked as a domestic.[24] John Charles Degagee, a Free African, hired himself as a seaman and was then able to pay "225 dollars for the freedom of his wife, Marie Virginie."[25]

Free black women did not limit their affections to free men; some also had relationships with slave men. The government's statistical officer, John Stobo, noted the situation of a woman who lived with a slave, did not work any grounds, and was entirely supported by him. Stobo also reported that the females of a group of manumitted slaves were "chiefly dependent on slaves for their support, seldom co-habiting for any length of time with one individual."[26] Another woman, Cottrine, a Free African, lived with Daniel Bruce, a slave, "whose ground she cultivated for subsistence and occasionally worked in cutting wood for fuel; and it appeared by working hard . . . she could earn two dollars a week to buy clothes." Free African women were, however, encouraged to marry either other Free Africans like themselves or free men of color so as not to hamper government efforts to settle them in "a better country than Tortola." A report is also made of a woman who was herself free and involved in huckstering but was "fed by her husband," a slave. Given the structure of plantation society, free women's relationships with slaves may have been seen as materially and socially inferior to relationships with white men or free black or colored men. It is also possible that free women with few attractive qualities were the ones who had to settle for relationships with slaves.

Little is known about how white and black women in the Virgin Islands related to each other or how the relationship between the two affected the status and condition of the latter. One observer noted that the "ladies of the Virgin Islands treat their slaves tenderly and hence no people in the West Indies are better obeyed than they."[27] This is contradicted by another writer who claimed that Creole women were "not the gentlest mistress," speaking "very imperiously" to their domestics.[28] Although it is difficult to say who was more likely to manumit their slaves, white men or white women, the list of white women who did so is quite long. White women in America were prominent abolitionists, and it is likely that their activism influenced at least some of their sisters in the Caribbean. Mention has already been made of Mirriam Harragin, but women such as Rachael Smith, who is recorded as freeing Harriet and her eight children "for the faithful service of mother," and Elizabeth Sewer, who freed three females for "love and affection," did exist. Hannah Abbot, Samuel Nottingham's sister, left her brother's manumitted slaves a legacy of £316.6.

No records have been found supporting the notion of sexual jealousy that many white women in other countries felt toward black women, though it likely existed. Certainly, the female relatives of white men with coloured mistresses must sometimes have felt humiliated by these liaisons. When "the only protector of a widowed mother and three maiden sisters" left home to form "a liaison . . . with a free woman of colour" his family could not have been too happy. The young man in this case ended up in jail after shooting his cousin, who was the lover of the young woman's sister.

Unfortunately, the violence of slave society sometimes found expression not only between whites and blacks but also between free and unfree blacks. The poverty of the people to whom many of the apprentices were assigned made their income-earning ability critical. When they did not deliver, the results could be violent. Dougan details one woman's experience:

I was urged by some Africans to witness the ill-treatment which their country-woman Ariange or Kate, apprentice of B. Rymer, a free woman of colour, was at the time receiving. I accordingly went to Mrs. Rymer's house, a small house of two rooms facing the street. On my inquiring for the mistress of the apprentice, a white man by the name of Coulter (living in a state of concubinage with Mrs. Rymer) opened the chamber door and exposed to my view the unfortunate apprentice, without any covering whatever. Her hands were tied over her head to a cross beam of the house, so as just to permit her to touch floor with her feet. She bore on her body marks of the chastisement given her by a cat, made of twisted cord which Coulter held in his hand and with which, he said, he had given her about a dozen lashes. The cause of this punishment, which Mrs. Rymer assigned, was, that the apprentice had been sent out to sell some bread, and that there was a deficiency in the returns.[29]

In another instance, a Free African woman placed with a free laundress whipped a slave to death for stealing from her. The former account, along with the story of Kitty, the slave beaten by Emmy, the driver woman, suggests that some black women may have felt little solidarity with each other. Slave women, the most vulnerable of all, lived under triple jeopardies. Enslaved plus black plus woman, they were the ones most abused under slavery by those with more power, however marginal.

WOMEN OF RESPECT: EXERTING INFLUENCE AND EXERCISING POWER

The planters created an image of the black woman antithetical to the idea of European "womanhood" as it was then understood. Unwittingly, they also created a space that allowed black women a degree of autonomy not available to their white sisters. In this space many black women created powerful and relatively autonomous roles for themselves within the slave community. Interestingly, the status some black women gained within both the slave and the free black communities mirrored those they could have been expected to assume in their villages back in Africa.

Some of the new arrivals from Africa, men and women, were obeah practitioners and could command the fear and obedience of their fellow slaves.[30] Most likely the amulets many slaves wore were protective fetishes made by obeah workers. In fact, obeah was used to prevent, detect, and punish crimes among the slaves and also served a medicinal purpose.

Illnesses common among slaves in the Virgin Islands included elephantiasis, leg ulcers, and fevers. These and other conditions were treated with castor oil, aloes, cassia occidentalis (wild coffee), geoffra inermis, and dolichos parrias, according to a report made to the Royal College of Physicians in London.[31] These were tropical plants whose medicinal uses could not have been known to Europeans originally. Their use reveals exactly how much the white planters and doctors relied on the knowledge of herbal remedies slaves brought with them from Africa. On their arrival in the Caribbean, Africans instantly recognized many of the plants they had known at home. Cassia occidentalis, for instance, had long been used on the continent to treat stomachaches, fever, ringworms, sore throats, wounds, dropsy, and other illnesses.

The obeah practitioner's knowledge of herbs and plants had another side. In late eighteenth-century Tortola, "obeah men and women were to be found on every estate, practising their juggling cheats and too often lending their aid [to rebellious slaves] by furnishing poisonous preparations by which . . . many and valuable lives of both Blacks and Whites were sacrificed."[32]

As obeah practitioners, slave and free women assumed an influential role in the black community. Obeah was a secret knowledge, practiced in the shadows of plantation society, and therefore outside the realm of European influence and understanding. Edwards warned that "the negroes, in general, whether Africans or Creoles, revere, consult and fear" the obeah man or woman. House slaves took more readily than field slaves to European customs and conventions in speech, dress, and religious worship, but this did not prevent them from using obeah or the knowledge of obeah practitioners. Domestics, many of whom were women, worked in close contact with whites and had the opportunity to administer obeah poisons to their masters and mistresses; hence Arthur Hodge's fears. According to Porter, "individuals and whole families have poison administered to them by their Domestics, which they obtained from these horrid wretches,"—the obeah workers.

Black women could also enter the slave elite as midwives. Midwives were just below the head overseer and the housekeeper in the slave hierarchy. In most instances, slaves gained status by their importance to the prosperity of the plantation. Successful midwives not only reduced the cost of employing a European doctor, they kept labor replacement costs down. Midwives contributed to plantation society with its patriarchal underpinnings, but also subverted it by using their skills as a source for their own empowerment.[33]

Where the government failed in welfare, women stepped in. Moody mentions Catharine Cruise, a free woman who looked after the orphans of African apprentices.

Black women in the Virgin Islands played a significant role in preserving their people's cultural heritage. Obeah was not the only means by which they retained and passed on the memory of Africa. Cooking is taboo for many African men; it was left to women to preserve this link to their heritage. They were the ones who collected the food the slave master doled out. Anonymous describes seeing black women congregated at one estate on Tortola to receive their weekly ration of provisions. Each woman received from three to five dried fish (he thought these came from Nova Scotia) and several quarts of ground maize. Wentworth gives a similar description. He records watching the women of a plantation gather to collect their biweekly allowance of provisions—"flour or meal made from the Indian corn, imported from America, and pickled herrings, which are usually shipped from England." According to him, slaves in skilled occupations, such as carpenters, coopers, and blacksmiths, got a greater allowance than others.

Responsible for collecting the food, black women were also the ones responsible for preparing the family meals. They supplemented the food distributed by the master with the produce they themselves grew. The importance of slaves' provision grounds in helping to round out their diet should not be underestimated. The fresh vegetables and starches they grew probably staved off severe malnutrition, since the food doled out by the estates was less than adequate to meet what we now know to be the requirements of a nutritious and balanced diet.

Black women prepared a variety of dishes redolent of their African heritage. Pepperpot, a stew made with red pepper, some form of meat, and other seasonings, was popular in the territory and elsewhere in the region. Toulama, a ground provision or starchy vegetable that, when grated, produces a starch similar to arrowroot, was also a favorite and was used to make fungi, a jellylike pudding. Fungi could also be made from cassava, which was a staple on the African continent. The word "fungi" itself is a strong indicator of Virgin Islanders' African heritage. In the Twi language *fugyee* means a soft mealy of boiled yam; in Kimbundu *funzi* means a "cassava mush;" and in Congo *fundi* means "flour or porridge." Ducknoor, once a common local favorite, is a sweetbread made with green corn, flour, coconuts, and other ingredients, then boiled in a banana leaf. This was originally a Twi dish, known in their language as "boiled maize bread." Foo-foo, "a soup of mashed plantains," with several West African sources and mentioned by Eadie a century later, would also have been prepared by Virgin Islands women during slavery. Clearly, the type of food eaten and the manner in which Virgin Islands women prepared it preserved and passed on the legacy of Africa to succeeding generations.

In song and dance it was also women who often took the lead. Porter writes that "women were the principal actors" in "the Comfoo dance . . . which, horridly indecent as it is . . . was the chief source of [slave] amusement" during Christmas celebrations and on the Sabbath. Though Allsop's *Dictionary of Caribbean English Usage* carries no reference to Comfoo, there is a notation on the *Comfa*, which was a dance of "vigorous body motion performed by one or two women to the beating of big drums intended to bring about spirit possession from which the promoters may draw some benefit." The description of these dances is too similar for them not to have had the same origin and purpose. Through this dance, women's public status and their significance as the inheritors of a role as ancient as the cultures from which they came was confirmed.[34] Their prominence in the dance signaled their significance as the keepers of African culture. Just as importantly, these dances were an interruption in their lives as slaves, acting as powerful reminders of past freedom. Unfortunately, Comfoo and other dances were the target of missionary activism and were on the decline by the time Porter wrote about them in the 1820s.

Though black women's leadership and involvement in their community's cultural life was extensive, it was their involvement in the territory's internal economy that sometimes led directly to their independence. In 1824, the government statistical officer reported that 2,933 enslaved men and women cultivated gardens for their own benefit.[35] But it was women who built up a huckstering business around what they and their partners grew.[36] In one report, mention is made of Diana, one of a group of manumitted slaves, whose partner, Jeffrey, a slave belonging to a Mr. Pickering, worked her grounds, assisted by hired slaves from Pickering's estate. Grounds requiring the use of so many additional hands suggest that Diana was involved in the biggest internal retail business of the time—huckstering.

The 1828 Blue Book for the Virgin Islands relates that "hucksters carry about goods in trays for sale. This traffic is carried on generally by female coloured persons and slaves." In fact, Dougan reported seeing many Free African women "at the intervals granted to them for their meals, bringing to town on their heads very heavy loads of wood, which they had collected for sale with a view of adding to their comforts and those of their children." Their huckstering allowed black women to earn money for their labor, which in turn allowed for a measure of economic and even physical freedom. It also allowed them to re-create a role that many might have played in their homeland. Amadiume points out that the Nnobi people of West Africa value industriousness, economic self-help, and self-sufficiency in women. A "good" Nnobi woman is expected to support the family through farming, marketing, and trading.[37] Many Virgin Islands women identified with this ideal. Their industry was all the more admirable, given that higglers walked "over steeps well-nigh perpendicular and by tracks, not roads, washed fearfully rugged by floods."

Blacks were never the happy-go-lucky slaves of popular pro-slavery imaginings. They wanted their freedom and wanted it badly, as can be inferred from these women's unrelenting hard work. Moody described the life of one huckster in the report published in the House of Commons Parliamentary Papers: "Christiana Wheatley lives by hucksterng corned fish, which she buys fresh and salts it. She buys three boneta fish, weighing about 12 lbs. for 12 dogs[38] and pays one dog for salt ... she is able to sell [the salted fish] for 15 dogs in the country."[39]

Some women conducted their business on behalf of their female owners. An observer noted that "women of colour go from door to door with large trays, on what bears every onus here, the head; in which are various articles of sale, generally the property of white ladies." Even the president's wife participated in this form of trading and had two women huckstering on her behalf.

Using black women to huckster for them allowed white women to remain on their pedestals, above the realm of "dirty" commerce. It was yet another area in which white women's dependence on the labor of black women revealed the distinctions between contemporary conceptions of what was appropriate to the womanhood of each race.

Huckstering throughout the islands was not the only avenue to retail business open to black women. Provisions, fish, straw baskets, and other goods were also sold weekly at the Sunday market in Road Town. Women would make their way to town before the sun had risen, holding their goods in bags and baskets steady on their heads. At the market, which lasted until noon, black women could forge important fraternal bonds with other women. There they affirmed and created social and business ties, creating, for at least a few hours each week, an identity separate from the plantation and from the institution of slavery. The fact that the only slaves who could leave the plantations without a pass were those going to market meant that some black women also enjoyed a level of mobility denied to many black men, since men were not as involved in this internal trade.

The market was, in fact, a very visible exhibition of black women's participation in the commercial and therefore public life of the islands. Tortola was in no way the commercial hub that nearby St. Thomas was. There were few shops. Huckstering, throughout the islands and at the Sunday market, was the dominant internal retail business of the time.

The higgling in general and the Sunday market in particular allowed black women to re-create, in an alien environment, a space that was familiar to them. The Nnobi women of West Africa monopolized the market space through their role in agricultural production and their control of the subsistence economy. They were the ones in charge of agricultural production and the ones who did the buying and selling. This was the norm throughout Africa.

That women were successful at marketing and other ventures may be inferred from the return of manumissions recorded in the Registry Office between 1 January 1825 and 1 October 1830. Of the forty-six slaves who paid for their own manumissions, twenty-eight were women, some of whom also paid for their children. One woman, Mary Taylor, paid for herself and for her mother.

Although some freed women encountered financial difficulties, it is clear that others were nevertheless able to establish small businesses. Not all were hucksters or petty merchants. A few opened boardinghouses or arranged to let out rooms. The House of Commons Parliamentary Papers mentions Sally Keys, a free colored woman in Road Town, at whose house one of the men investigating the status of slaves in the Virgin Islands stayed.[40] Keys, like the taxpayers mentioned below, was one of several slave-owning women who also were assigned Free African apprentices.

Some free women were able to parlay their cooking, midwifery, and other skills into ownership of land and slaves. Frances Slaney, a free colored woman from Road Town, is said to have bought a cotton plantation with the money she earned as a seamstress.

The will of Kitty Turnbull reveals just how extensive free black women's ownership of slaves could be.

I give to my Granddaughter Ann Maria Skerret my negro woman named Mary and her son named William with her future Issue and Increase—I give to my Grandaughter Catherine Scatliff (sic) my negro girl named Amelia daughter of the said Mary—I give my son Thomas William Audain my girl named Catey daughter of the said Mary—I give to my Sister Frances Audain my negro woman Bess who was the property of my late father William Turnbull—I give my said Son Thomas William Audain my negro woman Sophia—seven years after my decease I give my negro girl Zelpha her freedom and it is my desire that she shall be under the directions of my Daughter Catherine Fraser until the expiration of the said seven years—I desire that my negro woman Judy be sold and the money to be appropriated for the use of my Granddaughter Catherine Turnbull Audain.[41]

Interestingly, all but one of the slaves mentioned in the excerpted will quoted above are women or girls. (The son, William, may have been a young child.) Two, Amelia and Catey, are the daughters of Mary, but we do not know the provenance of the others. Kitty Turnbull's ownership of so many women could have reflected financial considerations—female slaves were cheaper than male slaves—or it could have been a symptom of other factors. Enslaved men could have been perceived as more difficult to control, particularly by a woman, and more prone to run away or rebel. Like white women, Turnbull probably put these slaves to work huckstering or hired them out as laundresses—jobs that were seen as the province of black women.

In 1823, there were only 269 free black and colored women in Road Town. The majority of free blacks, 463, lived in the country, but five years later the balance had shifted. According to the Blue Book for 1828, of the 738 free black and colored women, 410 lived in Road Town. As emancipation neared, more and more women were trying to find opportunities for themselves in town. Some may have found employment as hucksters, whereas others may have owned slaves who huckstered on their behalf. In those years, leading black and colored female taxpayers included Catharine Fraser (possibly the same woman mentioned in Kitty Turnbull's will), Sarah Hill, and Mary Walters. These women and about twenty-seven others like them paid an annual parish capitation tax on their slaves of 6s. each and also were taxed on the assessed value of their houses in Road Town. Thirty out of seventy-five free black taxpayers were women.

The fact that, to a significant extent, the internal Virgin Islands economy depended on black women hucksters, seamstresses, washers, and taxpayers did not translate into political power. The franchise was extended only to every "male, white, Protestant who was a free and natural born or naturalised subject of the British Crown and possessed in freehold ten acres of land or a house and land to the yearly value of 10 pounds." These restrictions along with the high level of planter absenteeism meant that political and official power resided in the hands of a few. Often one man served in several roles. Mark French was postmaster, king's counsel, estate attorney, justice of the peace, and more.

The situation also resulted in such bizarre elections as the one described by Anonymous. When elections were called on Jost Van Dyke to elect two white freeholders to the General Assembly on Tortola, "three sun-dried mortals declared the candidates who came with us to be unanimously chosen: they had good reason for saying as much, seeing themselves composed the whole body of constituents."

By 1815, free blacks in the Virgin Islands owned houses and land valued at £138,000 or nearly 20 percent of the total value of property. Already possessing some degree of economic power, free black men demanded and were granted a greater say in government. In 1818 they gained the right to elect a white freeholder as their representative to the Assembly. The extension of the franchise to black men began the gradual handing over of patriarchal power from white men to black men. By giving free black men the vote, white men admitted them, in however limited a way, to the arena of political participation. The political marginalization of women, black and white, continued, however. Their economic successes were not enough to help them transcend the gender barriers of their time.

NOTES

1. George Suckling, *An Historical Account of the Virgin Islands in the West Indies* (London: Benjamin White, 1780), p. 3.

2. George Truman, John Jackson, and Thomas B. Longstreth, *Narrative of a Visit to the West Indies* (New York, 1844; rpt., New York: Books for Libraries Press, 1972), p. 27.

3. Trelawney Wentworth, *The West India Sketch Book* (London: Whittaker and Co., 1834), p. 164.

4. Patterson notes that "among the mass of field slaves the highest post was that of driver." Orlando Patterson, *The Sociology of Slavery: An Analysis of the Origins, Development and Structure of Negro Slave Society in Jamaica* (Rutherford: Farleigh Dickinson University Press; London: Associated University Presses, 1969), p. 62.

5. Further testimony revealed that the slave woman, Kitty, was married to Emmy's son, Ben, which may have accounted for Emmy's hostility. *House of Commons Parliamentary Papers, 1826–27*, vol. 22, pp. 484–581.

6. Barry W. Higman, "The Slave Populations of the British Caribbean: Some Nineteenth Century Variations," in *Caribbean Slave Society and Economy: A Reader,* ed. Hilary Beckles and Verene Shepherd (Kingston: Ian Randle Publishers, 1991), pp. 221–225.

7. Samuel and Mary Nottingham manumitted their twenty-five slaves in 1784 and gave them fifty acres of land. John Stobo, *Government Statistical Report, 1824. CO 239/11.*

8. West Indian Agent to Lords Commissioner of Trade. *CO 232/2,* 1697. The agent was responding to a letter from the Board of Trade, which was seeking to find a colony to which they could deport a group of seven convict women.

9. Hilary Beckles, "Sex and Gender in the Historiography of Caribbean Slavery," in *Engendering History: Caribbean Women in Historical Perspective,* ed. Verene Shepherd, Bridget Brereton, and Barbara Bailey (Kingston: Ian Randle Publishers, 1995), p. 133.

10. Survey of Tortola by Robert Wilkinson. Rpt. 1985, Government of the Virgin Islands. Caribbean Printing Company. Interestingly, although the majority of plantations on Tortola grew sugar, three out of these four woman-owned estates grew cotton.

11. Report of Thomas Moody in *Slave Trade: Further Papers Relating to Captured Negroes,* House of Commons, 16 March 1825, p. 68. Major Thomas Moody and John Dougan were commissioned by the British Parliament to investigate the circumstances of all Africans in the Virgin Islands liberated from slaveships through the interception of slave traders.

12. Wentworth, p. 197.

13. As Beckles suggests, any imagery of black women that denied them feelings of maternalism also denied them any aspiration to "true" womanhood as realized by European women. It was, after all, in their dedication to motherhood that women were expected to find actualization. Beckles in Shepherd, *Engendering History*, p. 136.

14. Bryan Edwards, *The History, Civil and Commercial of the British West Indies, Vol. II* (London, 1819; rpt., New York: A.M.S. Press, 1966), p. 176.

15. In Elsa Goveia, *Slave Society in the British Leeward Islands at the End of the Eighteenth Century* (Puerto Rico: Institute of Caribbean Studies, University of Puerto Rico, 1965), p. 123.

16. Richard Watson, *A Defense of the Wesleyan Methodist Missions in the West Indies* (London: Thomas Cordeaux, 1817), p. 19.

17. Answer to Questions Proposed by Royal College of Physicians on 25 November 1829. *CO 239/22.*

18. John Stedman, quoted in Barbara Bush, *Slave Women in Caribbean Society 1650–1838* (Kingston: Heinemann Publishers [Caribbean], 1990), p. 25.

19. Mulattoes were seen as the natural allies of the whites. Goveia notes that "there was a strong social prejudice against employing "mixed blood" slaves in field work." Goveia, p. 231. Edwards argued that "greater privileges" should be accorded to the colored people "according to their approximation to the Whites." Edwards, p. 24.

20. James Johnston Abraham, *Lettsom, His Life, Times, Friends and Descendants* (London: William Heinemann Medical Books, 1933), p. 63.

21. John Stobo, *Government Statistical Report, 1824. CO 239/11.*

22. The Slave Act of the Virgin Islands required free blacks and coloreds to choose a "patron or protector" and register their choice with a magistrate. Commission of Legal Enquiry, 1826. *CO 318/64.* It is quite likely that those women not in a permanent relationship with a white man were at the sexual mercy of any male patron.

23. Thomas Southey, *Chronological History of the West Indies* (London, 1827; rpt., London: Frank Cass and Co., 1968) p. 501.

24. *House of Commons Parliamentary Papers, 1825*, vol. 25, pp. 566–663.

25. Report of William Dougan in *Slave Trade: Further Papers Relating to Captured Negroes*, House of Commons, 16 March 1825, p. 14.

26. Stobo, *CO 239/11*. Stobo often seemed determined to prove that blacks were better off as slaves than when freed, and his accounts must be read with that understanding. It is unlikely that the women Stobo refers to in the latter instance did not contribute in some way to their maintenance.

27. Suckling, p. 7.

28. Anonymous, *Letters from the Virgin Islands* (London: J. Van Voorst, 1843), p. 88.

29. Dougan, p. 10. The apprentice explained that some of the people to whom she'd sold the bread had not paid her.

30. No precise origin for the word "obeah" has been determined. The Ibibio word "abia," meaning a practitioner or herbalist, the Nembe "obi," meaning sickness or disease, and the Efik "ubio," meaning "a charm laid on the ground to cause sickness," suggest a strong West African connection. Richard Allsop, *Dictionary of Caribbean English Usage* (Oxford: Oxford University Press, 1996), p. 412.

31. Answer to questions proposed by the Royal College of Physicians, 6 February 1830, *CO 239/22.*

32. Porter Report, 1824, *CO 239/11.* For more on the paradox presented by the behavior of house slaves who used their favored positions to resist slavery, see Bush, p. 61.

33. This situation mirrored that of abolitionist women in Britain who used the movement to empower themselves even as male abolitionists argued for amelioration for female slaves on the basis of the frailty of their sex.

34. Patterson suggests that the aggression of the slaves found safe displacement in their dancing (Patterson, p. 248), but the fairly high frequency with which rebellions occurred in the Virgin Islands might indicate that they had the opposite effect.

35. Slaves also owned houses, horned cattle, goats, pigs, poultry, and boats. Stobo estimated the total value of their possessions at approximately £15,032. Report of Statistical Officer, *CO 239/11*.

36. Beckles details five basic types of female slave hucksters, ranging from plantation hucksters who sold food raised in their gardens on their own account to slave women who managed small retail shops on their owners' account. For more see Hilary Beckles, *Natural Rebels: A Social History of Enslaved Black Women in Barbados* (London: Zed Books, 1989), p. 79.

37. Ifi Amadiume, *Male Daughters, Female Husbands: Gender and Sex in an African Society* (London: Zed Books, 1987), pp. 39 and 94.

38. According to several sources, dogs were French copper coins struck in the reign of Louis XVI. Their value is variously given. In 1850, the value of a dog was equal to nine pennies sterling, but in 1860, the dog was said to be worth only three quarters of a penny. *House of Commons Parliamentary Papers, 1888*, vol. 72, Blue Book, 1850, *CO 317/21*. Blue Book, 1860, *CO 317/31*.

39. *House of Commons Parliamentary Papers, 1825*, vol. 25, pp. 664–759. Dougan's report on Christiana Wheatley differed from Moody's as quoted above. Dougan said she did well enough to send assorted vegetables and provisions to her grandmother on St. Croix. Dougan, p. 20, *Slave Trade: Further Papers Relating to Captured Negroes.*

40. *House of Commons Parliamentary Papers, 1825*, vol. 25, pp. 566–663. For more on black women as lodging house owners, see Paulette A. Kerr, "Victims or Strategists? Female Lodging House Keepers in Jamaica" in Shepherd, *Engendering History*, pp. 197–212.

41. Virgin Islands Historical Documents, vol. 1, no. 2. May–June 1984 (Tortola: Road Town Public Library, 1984), p. 3.

CHAPTER 2

—◆◆◆◆◆—

Amelioration

ABOLITIONISTS AND PATRIARCHY

The heyday of plantation society in the Virgin Islands coincided with a rise in missionary activity locally and with abolitionist zeal in London.

Though the Quakers had been the first to arrive (in the early 1720s), their presence had declined by the 1760s, and they did not have much impact on the slave population.[1] The Church of England arrived in 1745, but it was the established church and the church of the planter class. It ignored the slaves. According to a Methodist missionary, "the Anglican Clergy never considered the negroes as any part of their charge nor did they baptise either the newly imported slaves or those born in the colony, except a planter desired to have a favourite negro baptised." Indeed, at least two Church of England priests owned sugar estates and slaves on Tortola. Rev. T. Braithwaite in the late 1700s owned land at Sea Cows Bay and Kingstown, and Rev. James Wynne, an Episcopal minister resident in Scotland, had extensive holdings. He owned land on the western end of Tortola, at Carrot Bay, in the Mount Sage area and close to Fort Burt. A service at a church on Wynne's estate was described as being attended by half a dozen of the neighbouring planters with about "a score of Negroes, principally children, the black faces and sparkling eyes of the females set in relievo of their snow-white turbans."

Despite this evidence of racial inclusion, the Wesleyan Methodists had a much greater significance for blacks. In 1789, under the direction of Dr. Thomas Coke, Wesleyan missionaries established themselves on Tortola.[2] From the beginning they concentrated their efforts on the black population. By 1790 they could claim 900 colored and black members. Ten years later that number had risen to 3,000 coloreds and blacks and 117 whites. Membership dropped to 1,782 for blacks and coloreds and 62 for whites in 1820, but Methodist influence remained strong. The missionaries worked hard.

On the Sabbath-day we preach twice. . . . From four to six o'clock of the afternoon of the Sabbath-days we keep a school, where many of the free, coloured, and slave children, with some of the Africans are taught to read, spell, &c. On Tuesday, Thursday, and Saturday mornings, from sun rising to eight o'clock, we keep a school . . . on Thursday evening there is public preaching by one of the missionaries. On Friday evening there is a public catechetical meeting held . . . at these meetings one of the missionaries is always present, and either instructs the people in a catechetical manner, or gives a short lecture on some important Christian duty. On Saturday evening there is band meeting held, at which the more pious among our people receive instruction.[3]

Missionaries and planters alike emphasized the potential for religion to control the slaves and ensure their submissiveness. Caribbean missionaries were warned by the London Missionary Society that it would be "extremely wrong to insinuate anything which might render [the slaves] discontented with a state of servitude."[4] Slaves who were Methodists could be expelled from the church for disobedience to and running away from masters.[5] Indeed the missionaries often preached "about the duties of servants to their masters." Their efforts were appreciated. In 1830, a Tortola-based missionary wrote to London that "we have had during the year from the highest authorities in this Island the most flattering and public testimonials of the salutary effect of our labours in rendering the slaves under our attention Encreasingly steady, diligent and trust worthy in their Employment and as giving them a decided superiority over their fellows, both as to their general deportment and the extent and quality of their Labour."[6]

But black women as well as men found avenues for leadership within the church as exhorters and local preachers. Their advancement subverted the church's urgings to subservience. In fact, black women became the pillars of the church. Missionaries' letters and reports of the time are replete with allusions to their contributions to the spread and success of Methodism.

A Methodist missionary writing in 1806 described a church meeting in Virgin Gorda during which "one of the leaders told us that she had for some months a continual sense of the presence of God resting on her soul." Parliamentary Papers for 1826–1827 mention Rose Grimes, a free woman of color, a midwife, and "for many years one of the leaders of the Methodist Society." Certainly, the number of female leaders was often greater than that of male leaders. In 1834, there were forty-three female leaders on Tortola, but only twenty male leaders.[7] Leaders were "persons of the greatest piety and knowledge," each of whom took on the oversight and instruction of twelve to thirty men and women. They were responsible for the religious instruction of the faithful on Tuesday and Wednesday evenings and at other times when the missionaries were not present.

By allowing black women and men leadership roles within the church and by refusing to believe that religious instruction was beyond their understanding, missionaries sowed subversive seeds. On the one hand they preached subservience, but on the other they embraced converted blacks on a footing of near equality with whites. It is no wonder then that Methodist missionaries were implicated in at least two rebellions. Members of the Methodist society were among "a great number of slaves [who] revolted from their masters" in 1799. The Assembly on Tortola, composed of the territory's leading planters, summoned the Methodist missionaries at the time to determine their involvement. "The gentlemen on the Island became greatly alarmed, apprehending that the revolt which they beheld had resulted from those principles which had been inculcated among their slaves."[8] The missionaries agreed to prohibit meetings held in their absence, and the work of conversion continued.

Decades later Methodist missionaries again came under suspicion of inciting their congregations. In 1853, they were blamed for not doing enough to quell that year's rebellion. Some accused them of inciting it. The church's dedication to re-creating slave families in the image of patriarchal English families was thus overshadowed by the revolutionary impact of treating blacks like humans. The Methodist missionaries aimed to re-create among their converts the character and behavior of middle-class English Christians, people who were unquestionably free.

Yet beyond admitting blacks into the power structure of the church, the contribution of the Methodists to the people's development was most felt in the classroom. Since the local government made no provision for the education of slaves, churches served as schoolhouses. On weekdays, adults went to school in the evening after finishing their plantation work. Three days a week, children were taught from six to eight o'clock in the mornings before they joined the third gang. Children also attended school from four to six o'clock on Sunday afternoons. Basic as it was, the education offered by the missionaries was also attractive to women.[9] A missionary described "the adult female class in 1821 [as] consisting of girls and old women from the age of 18 to 100 years old." He added that "she who is said to be 100 showed much greater concern to learn the . . . catechism than younger ones." By 1833, there were 87 women and 255 girls in the Methodists' schools but only 17 men and 93 boys.

Women's school attendance is particularly remarkable given the scope of their plantation and home duties. Their enthusiasm for learning elicited praise. Dougan noted the "persevering assiduity of the females with young children in their arms, attending the school at early dawn during the hour which was allowed them for that purpose." Undoubtedly these women had a vision of future participation in a world that granted them the use of their education. They may not have known when this world would arrive, but they certainly intended to be ready for it. In 1830, a missionary wrote that

It has frequently been a source of great Encouragement to mark the rapid improvement of a few of the Female Adults. Five within the last four months have proceeded from a partial knowledge of their letters to an acquaintance with the New Testament and evince an Equal profit and Interest in perceiving the sacred volume. On these we have looked with fond expectation as the future hope and stay of our Infant Sunday School.[10]

Since women outnumbered men as students, it is no surprise that they also outnumbered men as teachers: teachers were eventually taken from the pool of students. The ratio of female teachers to male was often quite high. In 1833, for instance, the Methodists had thirty female teachers but only eight male teachers.

Some women went on to start their own schools. In a report on a group of forty-eight freed slaves, Stobo wrote that "one of the females can read and Grace Frett, wife of Jeffrey, keeps a school and has at present five pupils." Clearly, black women in the Virgin Islands had taken the lead in education.

SHAPING THE NEW WOMAN

Missionaries' influence was not as benign when it came to African cultural traditions as they survived on the plantation. Determined that Christianity should replace African spiritual practices and beliefs, they sought to eliminate and throw into disrepute those customs that, coincidentally, allowed black women a degree of sexual and economic freedom. Originally subjected to degraded and debased stereotypes that allowed planters access to her labor and her body, the black woman would now be remodeled in the image of the white woman. The new black woman was to reflect the traditional image of the chaste, subservient, dependent white woman.

The missionaries' "conception of the new black woman . . . [thus] focused on marriage, child rearing and domestic duties."[11] Missionaries and abolitionists set about to encourage slaves to adopt Christian marriage and to persuade slave owners to encourage monogamy. Methodist missionaries were told to perform the ceremony of marriage among their slave members as well as among those who sought to become members. Under the Leewards Islands Melioration Act of 1798, the "marriage of slaves [could not] give any particular rights either to the contracting partier or their children." Nevertheless, missionaries claimed that "although [the ceremonies they performed] were not formally recognized by the law, they were, not-withstanding regarded as morally good and binding and were productive of very salutary effects."[12]

Through the efforts of the missionaries and abolitionists, legislation was passed that sought to ease black women's condition on the plantations. The 1798 amelioration code mentioned above, lobbied for by the abolitionists, required owners to give each woman in a monogamous union a certain amount of money for each of her live births.[13] It also required a white man convicted of intercourse with a married female slave to pay a fine of £100. (By this time much had been written speculating that slave women's low fertility could be traced to their alleged promiscuity and to the "prevalence of concubinage with white masters."[14] In the face of abolitionist agitation against the continuation of the slave trade, planters became more interested in furthering natural increase.)

In an 1823 circular despatch, the Secretary of State for the Colonies, Lord Bathurst wrote:

The system of meliorating the condition of slaves . . . cannot better commence than by the adoption of a principle which by making a distinction of treatment between the male and female slaves cannot fail to raise this unfortunate class generally above their present degraded level and to restore to the female slaves that sense of shame which is at once the ornament and the protection of their sex and which their present mode of punishment has tended unfortunately to weaken if not to obliterate.[15]

A Consolidated Order in Council issued by Her Majesty's government for promulgation throughout the British West Indies forbade the flogging or whipping of female slaves. Further, marriages were to be encouraged and the separation of families by sale was prohibited.

By 1830, planters were also forbidden to put pregnant women to heavy work or to subject them to any punishment except imprisonment. Slave women who had six or more children were supposed to be permanently exempted from hard labor. The private world of the colonial plantation where planters had been allowed carte blanche bowed to that of the public, political, and external world as represented by the British Parliament.

Many women embraced the concept of Christian marriage. A guest describes the wedding ceremony of one Tortolian couple.

The bridegroom, Lancaster Stevens . . . had procured a license gratis, although this mystery is wont to extract a doubloon from the pockets of less fortunate suitors. His reason for seeking one . . . [was] that missey, being an heiress in her way, desired to be espoused otherwise than the Guinea niggers; these are the African slaves whose marriages always take place by banns and are celebrated in open church; they are held in much contempt here. Accordingly at seven at night, lights duly arranged in Lancaster's neat cabin showed a motley assemblage; His Honour and the clerk of the council, the clerk in orders and the parish clerk being the chief dignitaries in presence.

There were bon-bons on a sideboard . . . two circular cakes, one plain, its neigh-
bour frosted, with delicious little parti-coloured imps figuring on the top and both
having miniature British silk flags waving over them. All around tempted to allay
any thirst they might create:-cold punch, sack, noyau, or eke porter-cup for those
entitled to entrance; with Spanish brandy to enliven the rabble out doors.[16]

According to this writer, the bride's "snowy attire" included satin shoes,
silk hose, and an "ample white veil." Marriage and the manner in which the
wedding ceremony itself occurred was perceived by many in the black
community to confer respectability and status.

But even in slavery, African women had gained a degree of sexual and
even economic freedom. Some had forged positions of leadership within
the slave system as it existed prior to the efforts of the abolitionists. As
hucksters some were businesswomen who would not have appreciated
missionaries' efforts to end the Sunday market to allow for church attendance. And, however powerful the ideology of marriage, many did not rel-
ish relinquishing their freedom to become mere wives after the European
model. Slavery had put black women under the often-remote mastery of
white men. Black men had no legal rights over their women, and slave
women did not depend on them for their maintenance.[17] In this environment women could express their sexual freedom by terminating unsatis-
factory unions at will. Men and women "agreed to live together as man and
wife: they cohabited until one was tired and then parted and formed other
connexions [sic]. Sometimes a man had several wives at the same time and
the woman had many husbands successively so that every child had a different father."[18]

Free black women's economic power allowed them to demonstrate a degree of sexual freedom or choice denied to white women. Moody wrote of a
male slave manumitted by "a free female of colour [who] had taken a liking
to him and had purchased and manumitted him." The couple then proceeded to live together.

Many black women recognized that the Christian requirement of female
submission and loyalty to husbands would not only restrict these freedoms
but could also place them in physical jeopardy. This was not an unfounded
fear. Reports of domestic violence in those years are not hard to find. In
1783, a Virgin Islands court recommended that George Grundy be granted
mercy for the murder of his wife since

it was not committed from any premeditated malice but that it was the sudden im-
pulse of passion, occasioned by his wife giving him provoking language at the time,
and she was at that time drunk, that she had been frequently drunk before and was
always at such times very abusive, that there was not a weapon made use of, but the
blows she received . . . were made with his fist and that her drunkenness and rolling
down a hill might have been partly the occasion of her death.[19]

In short, she asked for it and was to blame. Though Grundy was found guilty and condemned to death, the recommendation of mercy secured him the king's pardon in 1784. The very fact that the race of this couple is not specified suggests that they were white, as does the fact that the case was brought to the attention of the Colonial Secretary, Lord Sydney. Black women would not have missed the underlying message that if white women could expect so little justice from the state, black women would receive even less, many being mere chattel who had no recourse to the law.

Contemporary observers noted instances of domestic abuse. Parliamentary Papers record the case of Cottrine, a Free African, whose collarbone was broken by the free colored man with whom she had lived. If she had been married and thus required by the dictates of church dogma to remain with the man, she may very well have been murdered. Another account of abuse reveals that "Daniel broke his wife, Phoebe's nose with a stick because she did not give him any money to buy clothes and victuals as the wives of other African apprentices did." [20]

Far from depending on men for their maintenance, the latter incident serves to show that women were often the ones who assumed the role of breadwinner. As noted previously, this reflected women's traditional roles in many African societies. If a Nnobi woman's husband was unable to provide money for food, she was expected to support the family from her crop cultivation and marketing efforts.[21]

By attacking the Sunday market and the cultural practices of the slaves, the missionaries hit directly at the sources of black women's empowerment.[22] They had no choice. If they were to ensconce the black man as the head of the family and persuade women of their inferiority, those factors that increased women's power had to be eradicated.

But the pre-abolition efforts of the missionaries to effect changes aimed at imposing patriarchal Christian notions of virtue and morality achieved only uneven results. A Tortola-based missionary wrote to his superiors that "since last February we have expelled hundreds for improper and immoral conduct and many of them for crimes of the grossest nature such as Drunkenness, Theft, Adultery, Fornication, Fighting, Lying and Swearing."[23] Moody later noted that at the time of his investigations, sixteen women had been expelled from society for "immorality of conduct."

Some church officials blamed the lack of women missionaries for the failure to effect the widespread adoption of stereotypical roles among black West Indian women.

An official sent out by the Missionary Society in the early 1800s believed that "there is a need for trained women workers. Our schedule shows that in all our churches women greatly outnumber the men. . . . The majority of our women members and adherents are of the labouring class and many of them greatly need instruction in the common duties of life in order that they may be better home-makers and mothers."[24]

Black women did not conform to prevalent European views on "womanhood." The standards met by white middle-class European women had been undermined from the very beginning by the demands of the plantation economy. Efforts to undo the damage were now seen to require the assistance of white women, who were expected to help black women become more like them. The absence of women missionaries in any large number short-circuited these hopes.

Because old habits die hard, planters also subverted missionaries' efforts to effect the feminization of black women along European lines. According to the House of Commons Parliamentary Papers for 1826 to 1827, there was ample evidence that female Liberated Africans indented for domestic work in the Virgin Islands were instead being sent to do field work. A report of the proceedings against a planter charged with sending four of these women to clear land stated that "it was expressly forbidden, both by the Order in Council and by the indenture of apprenticeship, to employ female apprentices in labours of agriculture on any account."[25] Hard economic concerns and the custom of many years militated against planters' full support for amelioration. Accustomed to considering black women the equals of black men in terms of their physical capabilities, planters found it hard to readjust their thinking and allow black women participation in concepts of European womanhood. Their recalcitrance made the work of missionaries harder.

Despite these obstacles some contemporary observers credited missionaries with many successes. Porter wrote in 1823 that "a great reformation . . . is evident among the people." He crowed that "Comfoo dances have been wholly abolished and obeah men and women are scarcely to be found [and] hundreds of men and women, decently, nay well dressed, regularly attend divine service in the Methodist Chapel."[26] But these loyal parishioners were resisting the cornerstone of missionary efforts. The marriage rate in the Virgin Islands remained low.[27] As late as 1846, the report of the stipendiary magistrate for the first half of that year recorded only five marriages performed by the established Church and fourteen by Wesleyan ministers. The numbers remained fairly stable until the end of the nineteenth century, with the Methodists reporting more success in marrying off their converts. Nevertheless, the majority of blacks consistently held back from making this substantive commitment to Christianity.

The reluctance of many to join the church probably was owing in no small part to the fact that blacks may have perceived Christianity as simply making flunkeys out of converts. One missionary noted that "many of our Negroes have by their merit obtained places of trust upon the estates as drivers, boilers, watchmen &c and some, especially in the island of Tortola, have supplied the place of white overseers." Opposition to religious conversion may, in reality, have been opposition to seeing some slaves becoming "more equal" than others.

Rules prohibiting contact between members in the Methodist Society and those who were living in sin, family or not, may also have turned many away. "Mothers receiving support from daughters living in concubinage with white, coloured or black men or countenancing them in any way in their iniquity cannot be in society," warned the Methodists' Notes on the Admission and Exclusion of Members. It added that "all our members are to be warned against visiting such persons or being intimate with them."[28]

Religion also divided men and women. The man who had been living with Cambric Dracott, a slave woman, upon her conversion to Methodism, "immediately became her enemy and stripped her of all she had ... leaving her much in debt." In fact, the Standing Rules of the Methodist Society prohibited anybody from becoming a member or communicant who was living in concubinage. "Nor can any who are Church members be allowed to remain in the number of communicants should they enter into the State of concubinage." Yet concubinage was fostered and encouraged in West Indian plantation society. Planters routinely took slave or free colored mistresses in addition to their wives, they split slave families, and, at least in the early days of slavery, they encouraged polygamy. The very foundation and structure of plantation society could not sustain church rules.

As the church through its teachings on monogamy, concubinage, and so on attempted to turn plantation society against itself, it pitted believers against unbelievers, free against unfree, and those who submitted against those who did not. Rose Grimes is reported as having testified on behalf of a planter accused of ill treating his African apprentices. She described the four women who had run away from him (and from previous masters) as "bad girls."[29] Her conversion probably encouraged her to perceive the women, newly come from Africa, as heathens and savages who did not understand their duty to their masters.

Undeniably the church, particularly the Methodist Church, brought some benefit to blacks. Church-initiated schools gave blacks the rudiments of an education previously denied them. Even the mere act of accepting blacks into the church, of evincing the belief that God's word should also be known to slaves, was revolutionary. It signaled a fundamental belief that blacks too could share in the fellowship of God. But what was given with one hand was taken away with the other. Blacks could partake of the benefits of church membership only on terms that denied them both their culture and the reflection of a God in their image. As the process of creolization and conversion continued in the post-emancipation era, many of the practices and beliefs that were the legacy of Africa slipped into the shadows of history. Along with them went an understanding and appreciation of women's roles in cultural customs that was only partially supplanted by their new roles in the church.

NOTES

1. Though Quakers in the Virgin Islands were prominent slave owners and often manumitted their slaves and ceded property to them, they seem to have concentrated their antislavery activity in London.

2. Thomas Coke, *A History of the West Indies Containing the Natural, Civil and Ecclesiastical History of Each Island* (1811; rpt., London: Frank Cass and Co., 1971), p. 111.

3. Report of William Dougan in *Slave Trade: Further Papers Relating to Captured Negroes*, House of Commons, 16 March 1825, p. 30.

4. "Instructions Given by the London Missionary Society to the Missionaries in the West Indies, 1812" in *British Colonial Development 1774–1834, Select Documents*, ed. Vincent Harlow and Frederick Madden (London: Oxford at the Clarendon Press, 1953), p. 549.

5. Letter from Thomas Harrison, 7 October 1824. *Wesleyan Methodist Missionary Society*, West Indies Correspondence General, 1824–1827.

6. Letter from John Burton, 15 January 1830. *Wesleyan Methodist Missionary Society, W.I. Correspondence General, 1828–1830.*

7. "Minutes of the District Meeting Commenced on Saturday the 1st day of February in the town of Basseterre, St. Christopher." *Wesleyan Methodist Missionary Society, W. I. Synod Minutes 1822–1838.*

8. Coke, p. 124.

9. Of course, the classroom was the perfect site for indoctrination into gender roles. Although both boys and girls at the National School in Road Town were given religious instruction and taught reading and spelling, boys were taught writing and arithmetic, whereas girls were educated in needlework. The very separation of the classes—girls were taught by a woman and boys by a man—would have sent a powerful message; men and women might work together in the fields, but in the classroom, the sexes were considered to have different capacities. At the National School, girls had to pass through only four classes; boys were expected to go through six forms. Account of Subjects Taught at National School, 10 October 1830. *CO 239/22.*

10. Letter from John Burton, 15 January 1830. *Wesleyan Methodist Missionary Society, West Indies Correspondence General 1828–1830.*

11. Catherine Hall, "Gender Politics and Imperial Politics: Rethinking the Histories of Empire," in *Engendering History: Caribbean Women in Historical Perspective*, ed. Verene Shepherd, Bridget Brereton, and Barbara Bailey (Kingston: Ian Randle Publishers, 1995), p. 56.

12. Letter from Methodist Missionary Commission to the secretary of state, 1836. In Blackman, p. 135.

13. Elsa Goveia, *Slave Society in the British Leeward Islands at the End of the Eighteenth Century* (Puerto Rico: Institute of Caribbean Studies, University of Puerto Rico, 1965), p. 196.

14. Harlow and Madden, p. 540.

15. Harlow and Madden, p. 561.

16. Anonymous, letters from the Virgin Islands (London: J. Van Voorst, 1843), p. 51.

17. As has been discussed, evidence exists to suggest, however, that some *freed* black women depended on slave men for their maintenance.

18. Richard Watson, *A Defense of Wesleyan Methodist Missions in the West Indies* (London: Thomas Cordeaux, 1817), p. 39.

19. President George Nibbs to Governor Shirley, 20 October 1783. *CO 152/63*.

20. *Parliamentary Papers, 1825*, vol. 25, p. 566–663.

21. Ifi Amadiume, *Male Daughters, Female Husbands: Gender and Sex in an African Society* (London: Zed Books, 1987), p. 94.

22. The situation found its parallel in West Africa, where, according to Miles, "white colonialists . . . systematically set about suppressing the market women." Rosalind Miles, *The Women's History of the World* (London: Penguin Group, 1988), p. 175. In the Virgin Islands, the move to abolish the Sunday market may have failed because it was spearheaded by the missionaries, who received only luke- warm support from other, more powerful whites.

23. Letter from Thomas Harrison, 9 September 1824. Wesleyan Methodist Mis- sionary Society, West Indies Correspondence, 1824–1827.

24. F. Deaville Walker, *The Call of the West Indies* (London: The Cargate Press of the Methodist Missionary Society, n.d.), p. 187.

25. *House of Commons Parliamentary Papers, 1826–1827*. Report of Captured Ne- groes, 11 June 1827, pp. 386–483.

26. Porter Report, 1824. *CO 239/11*.

27. Further, one missionary on Tortola lamented in 1824 that he had "never met with so many . . . instances of the violation of the marriage vow." Letter from Thomas Harrison, 7 October 1824. *Wesleyan Methodist Missionary Society, WI Corre- spondence General, 1824–1827*.

28. *Wesleyan Methodist Missionary Society Correspondence General, 1828–1830*.

29. *Parliamentary Papers, 1826–1827*, pp. 386–483.

CHAPTER 3

Post-Abolition Virgin Islands Society

EMANCIPATION AND ITS IMMEDIATE AFTERMATH

On 6 September 1831, an act was passed in the Virgin Islands declaring that "all Her Majesty's subjects . . . should be placed on the same footing without any complexional differences or distinction."[1] Free people of color, both men and women, could now own as many slaves as they pleased (before, they were restricted to fifteen) and did not have to pay higher taxes for land and property. But when it came to the territory's political life, the act very clearly spoke to racial difference; gender differences remained intact.

The same rights and privileges of public action and interaction accorded to white men were accorded to black and colored men. They could now not only vote but also run for office and serve on juries. The act swept away the barriers of race as if race were the only obstacle faced by those wishing to participate in the public sphere. In fact, by undoing the racial divisions between men, the act's language made clear women's absence from the public sphere of colonial life. The report of a Mr. A. Harrigan who "appeared and claimed for himself" the right to vote on the basis of property that actually belonged to a woman highlights women's subordinate status. They were subject to taxes but allowed no representation. The advantages free black women gained from the new act were solely economic in nature, allowing them to own more slaves and providing some ease from burdensome taxes.

The 1831 act also paved the way for the subsequent abolition of slavery in 1834. Emancipation came with little opposition in the Virgin Islands, and 1 August 1834, was a quiet day in the territory. Observers reported that some blacks spent the day attending church services, and it is likely that it was the missionaries who made the emancipation announcement in churches throughout the islands.

Many planters had already left the islands by the 1830s.[2] Some who remained may have felt a strong sense of complacency; except for plantation work, the emancipated slaves were not generally expected to find paid employment in the territory. Neither were they expected to do well on their own. Reports on the conditions of manumitted slaves and Free Africans or African apprentices often suggested that many were barely able to support themselves. In 1824 the government statistical officer wrote that of the twenty-five Nottingham slaves freed in 1784, there were only six survivors (all women) who, along with their families, "find it difficult to support themselves in dry years." In another account, the free Creole mistress of a Free African woman is quoted as saying that the woman would not be able to support herself if liberated because she wouldn't cultivate her grounds if free from the coercion of apprenticeship. The Creole mistress was herself described as poor.

Of course, prevailing gender and racial ideologies may have interacted in the above reports to promote the view that women were incapable of providing a living for themselves in the absence of a man, particularly a white man, i.e., the slave master.

A total of 1,944 men and 2,207 women were freed at emancipation. Between 1834 and the uprising of 1853, the majority of these formerly enslaved people remained on the plantations, working for the same masters and living in the same homes. Plantation owners and managers made contracts with their laborers specifying the nature of the work expected, wages, and other conditions. The Parliamentary Papers of 1839 record one such agreement between a J. B. Nibbs and his field laborers, who were "to enjoy the occupation of several houses and the use of provision grounds and to keep a reasonable number of stock and to be paid in cash." Both women and men were to receive one pound and seven and a half pennies per week in wages.

By the early 1840s the depressed prices sugar was fetching in Britain conspired with a series of hurricanes to drive wages down in the Virgin Islands. By 1845, only 900 men and women were working on the thirty sugar estates still functioning on Tortola, making between six and nine shillings per week.[3] Many of the laborers were required to pay rent out of their wages. In addition, missing a day's work often meant forgoing their salary for the entire week.

In 1846, the Stipendiary Magistrate brought the situation to the attention of the governor in Antigua, who, in turn, brought it up with the Secretary of State for the Colonies.

I regret to find that the labourer requires more protection than he at present enjoys when cultivating under the system of sharing the profits with the proprietor. I shall not fail to call Mr. Drummond Hay's[4] attention to this subject and I trust the legislature of the Virgin Islands will pass such an enactment in reference to the due performance of contracts, as may encourage the growth of that mutual confidence without which the share system cannot possibly succeed.[5]

The political discord following Drummond Hay's dissolution of the legislature that October conveniently prevented action on the above, however. A year later, conditions on the estates had deteriorated still further and it was reported that "very little money is being paid in wages now [and many] labourers work only two days in the week giving that labour as rent for their cottages and provision grounds." If they were required to work for more days, payment was expected on the share system, in which the planter placed his equipment and land at their disposal and gave them half of the resulting crop. This system did not function to laborers' advantage; it was not uncommon for planters to withhold laborers' shares after manufacture. Men and women still connected to the estates fought back with "petty acts of injury and spoil." These probably took much the same form as they had during slavery, i.e., destruction of cane, destruction of the sugar works, and contamination of water supplies.

Many laborers went to work for themselves.

In 1841, the Stipendiary Magistrate explained that "individual instances occur of labourers renting small portions of land upon which they settle withdrawing . . . from the cultivation of the staple product and giving their attention to the culture of ground provisions for sale or barter, to the care and pasturage of horned cattle, sheep and goats and the burning of lime principally for the St. Thomas market."

This spirit of self-reliance and independence was to become a characteristic of Virgin Islanders.

On Virgin Gorda some laborers found work with the Virgin Gorda Mining Company, which was working the copper veins there. The company employed "upwards of sixty women and children" and more than a hundred men.

Other laborers left their islands in search of work. The census of 1859 records that there were 431 "temporary absentees" at the time the census was taken. Of these, 173 were women. Many went no farther than the nearby Danish islands. According to one report "a large number of the labouring population" was now finding work on St. Thomas. St. Croix planters also turned to the Virgin Islands to find workers for their sugar plantations.[6]

Laborers' desertion to work their own land or to work on another island was regarded with extreme hostility by the planters. Some used violent coercion to try to prevent the exodus.

Some time ago Mr. Hunter pulled the trash[7] off and took away the doors and window from the house in which Fanny Anderson and her husband Virgil were living. This he did because Joan Anderson [her daughter] had gone to St. Thomas [to look for work]. [When she returned] Joan went to work at Cane Garden Bay. Mr. Hunter said she must come to work at Anderson's or he would turn [her parents off]. He had Joan's ground rooted up because she again went to St. Thomas.[8]

Not all the tactics used to get the freed blacks to remain on the plantations were as aggressive. The men and women who moved off the estates had to contend with a tax system designed by the planter-dominated Assembly to stop them from leaving the plantations. The Virgin Islands Tax Bill of 1840 imposed a twelve-shilling tax on every acre of provision grounds not attached to a plantation with an additional tax of 5 percent on any profit made therefrom. (It is worth remembering that by 1823, free coloreds and free blacks owned approximately 2,300 acres, 69 acres of which were under crop. One thousand three hundred acres was used as pasture land, and the rest was forest.)

Virgin Islanders protested the unfair taxation, but their grievances received short shrift from President H. Drummond Hay.[9] In a letter to Governor MacPhail written on 25 September 1840, he complained that "the portion of the community who suffer from [these taxes] are in general an idle race of persons who subsist from day to day on the produce of a patch of ground which they barely cultivate." The colonial authority in the Leeward Islands was more sympathetic to the newly freed blacks. MacPhail wrote Drummond Hay back, urging the repeal of tax laws "which fetter the exertions of the industrious and deserving labourers." It is unclear whether Drummond Hay did as asked, but his intractability on other matters might suggest that he would have felt no great urgency to do so.

Nevertheless, among the 900 laborers reported in 1843, 505 were taxpayers, owning between them 783 cattle and at least 15 horses. Most owned hogs and goats.

At emancipation the former slaves must have expected a substantial change in their material conditions. Instead, coercive tactics were employed to keep them on the estates at nearly nonexistent wages. If they moved off the estates, their provision grounds were subject to levels of taxation that hardly made the land worth cultivating. Their dissatisfaction and resentment grew. Faced with a hostile and unsympathetic president, many began to feel that direct action was necessary to better their circumstances. The passage in July 1853 of an amendment to raise the cattle tax was the last straw. The rumblings of discontent grew louder. The members of the Board of the Privy Council did not initially take the threat of rebellion seriously.

Instead, the board, meeting in Road Town, urged on 1 August that "the Wesleyan Ministers be requested to use their influence to allay the present agitation and to induce them to conform to the [cattle tax] law." The missionaries, Robert Hawkins and Joshua Jordan, did call a meeting, but they had their own agenda. They were fed up with what they called "an unparalled system of Taxation imposed upon the Wesleyan Methodist Missionary Society in the Virgin Islands." They were paying taxes on their mission houses, their horse, *and* their boat. Their chapel keeper was also taxed. The missionaries had applied for waivers, but these had not been considered by the House of Assembly, and the Crown was giving them no help.

Though no records of the actual meeting called by the missionaries have been found, it is safe to say that it did not have the calming effect the board had been hoping for. Afterward, more than a thousand men, women, and children marched through Road Town, the men armed with guns and the women and children with clubs. According to this same report, the marchers intended to "destroy all the white and coloured inhabitants."[10] Their anger seems to have been particularly directed at the special constables, many of whom may have been colored. (A 1793 act had created a corps of free colored infantry with white officers.)

The rioters had apparently had enough of an administration that did nothing to protect them from their bosses but that was taxing them into further poverty. "They want no President, no House of Assembly, no Custom House, only their Minister," reported the president. Despite their show of arms, the demonstration on the first day was peaceable. Violence came on the second day when one of the demonstrators was shot by a special constable defending the house of an Assembly member. By the next day the president reported that half the town lay "in total ruin" and that all the white families had left, escaping to St. Thomas. Besides President Thomas Chads, only the Wesleyan preacher, the doctor, and one other white remained on Tortola.[11]

The uprising, like the others that went before, was a spontaneous eruption on the part of the people, and the reports do not speak of any clear leader.[12] Though it was quickly over, its repercussions were felt well into the next century. In 1842 the population stood at 6,689; by 1859, it had dropped to 6,053. Many whites returned immediately after the 1853 uprising (the 1859 census records the presence of 201), but the exodus was under way and was to gather steam in the next decade.

The passage of the West Indies Encumbered Estates Act in 1864 sounded the death knell for plantation society in the Virgin Islands. The act allowed for the sale of encumbered estates and provided for easier land transfers. With hundreds of acres of land falling into black hands and with blacks' escalating exodus from what estates remained, any reason whites may have had for staying on disappeared. With the demise of slavery, many whites felt that the Virgin Islands had again become valueless.

Hurricanes, the departure of labor, and low sugar prices took their toll. Seven estates received relief advances from government in 1867. That number rose by two in 1868 with the estates receiving between £75 to £300. By 1879, there were 123 whites in the Virgin Islands. Two years later that number had decreased to 52. Their departure set the stage for a reversal of the political gains the islands had made since 1773.

POST-ABOLITION GOVERNMENT

Almost from the inception of civil government in the Virgin Islands, complaints were made about the poor caliber of Englishmen available to serve in leadership posts. Less than a handful of plantation owners were resident in the territory, and the situation elicited frequent comment.[13] "The only persons whose public services as Members of the Assembly can be procured are, for the most part, needy and adventurous, deficient alike in education, in decent habits of life, in suitable means of living and in status in society.... There is not proper material in the Virgin Islands to constitute a representative legislature."[14]

In 1854, a constitutional amendment act abolished the council and Assembly, replacing them with a legislature of ten members, of which only six would be elected. Voters had to be male British subjects who were £5 freeholders, £10 leaseholders, or £5 householders. In 1855 there were 139 registered voters, but by 1858 there were only 23. That the intention of the amendment was to limit the voting power black men gained in 1831 is clear. An 1858 report stated that "on the 30th day of June ... a large number of the inhabitants of the Virgin Islands attended at the Court House to record their votes when many were prohibited from recording their names it having been alleged by one of the Magistrates officiating that unless any individual approaching the record was in actual receipt of £5 per annum he could not vote."[15]

There appears to have been no outbreak of trouble on that occasion, but it would have served as a warning to colonial officials. Black men were eager to participate in politics. Colonial officials concluded that the room for political participation required further shrinkage. In 1859, just five years after the last amendment, the constitution was changed to provide for a Legislative Council of three nominated and four elected members presided over by the president. A year later, only ten out of forty-two registered electors were said to have voted, demonstrating the chilling effect the changes to the constitution was having.

Exacerbated by the size of the territory and absenteeism, the restriction of political power to the propertied meant that official positions were restricted to the men of only a few families. The incestuous nepotism of Virgin Islands government, long a feature of island life, attracted some concern on the part of President Thomas Price. In the 1850s he fired off a series of letters to Governor Hamilton about the situation. "The Provost Marshall, Mr. G. Gordon is 56 years of age and an older brother of the Chief Justice, his tenure of the Marshall's Office dates from 13 years ago. Previously he was a magistrate and member of the Council. His father as well as his brother was Chief Justice."

A follow-up letter pointed out that "the Colonial Secretary Mr. G.H.A. Porter . . . has held his present office since 1844. His father was Senior Member of Council . . . and Chief Justice. The father of the late Mr. G. K. Porter of the Board of Trade was a brother of the last named gentleman."[16]

Although the situation upset Price, it bothered no one else. The presidents and colonial officials who followed were more concerned about what President Arthur Rumbold called the "scarcity of men of sufficient intelligence . . . or who are even competent to exercise the election franchise."[17] Rumbold's opinion persuaded Governor Pine to conclude by the end of the year that "it may . . . be the case in the Virgin Islands . . . that the retention of the elective franchise tends to engender strife, falsehood and corruption." The passage of the Colonial Laws Validity Act in 1865 must have reassured these colonial officials about the impotence of colonial legislatures, which were elected by and included such dangerous men: the act voided any local legislation "repugnant to Acts of Parliament." Clearly, British colonial authorities wanted to create considerable distance between government and governed, especially if the two were in danger of coinciding in black men. Blacks in charge of themselves and their destiny could not be accommodated within a colonial empire built on the subjugation of colored people. Virgin Islands women, which, by that time, was to say black women, lived at an even more distant remove from the state. They were excluded from the political arena not only by living in a racist colonialist society but also by their sex. As women they were expected to be represented by their men in the polity. European patriarchal thought held that women had the status of children in public life—they should neither be seen nor heard. It was this ideology of male domination that held sway in the colonies and that ensured that whatever equality black men and women had experienced in the field during slavery would not extend to public life. But political advancement for black men was under siege. When it seemed that a few concessions to elite black men would allow plantation society to continue almost undisturbed, colonial authorities had made those concessions. But the exodus of blacks from the estates, the fall in sugar prices, and the uprising of 1853 all led to an unforeseen abandonment of the Virgin Islands by whites. Faced with the prospect of a black-governed colony, colonial authorities worked themselves into a fever trying to reverse the gains previously made by black men.

The campaign to completely remove the franchise from the ranks of the new electorate gathered steam in 1867. Rumbold complained to Pine that "the community is composed almost exclusively of peasants or labourers [who are] . . . totally unfitted for popular or representative institutions." According to him, the abrogation of the elective franchise was necessary for the "protection of property and enterprise."[18] Rumbold's repeated pleas on the subject produced results by the middle of 1867, when full Crown Colony government was introduced into the territory. The Legislative Council was reduced to six nonelected members. These members included the president or commissioner, the colonial secretary, the colonial treasurer, and three unofficial members nominated by the president.

The passage from elective to Crown Colony government did not pass unremarked or unprotested; more than a hundred men memorialized the queen, petitioning for the restoration of the franchise. Though some signed with X's, their action suggests that many recognized what was being lost.

Although emancipation brought a nominal freedom, the repeated changes to the constitution made clear the British position that the former slaves and their descendants could not aspire to political maturity. By removing the vote and removing the possibility of political advancement, blacks were kept in a state of political infantilism. In a sense black men were the ones who lost the most since it was they who had made the initial advance into the polity. Not only had they received the vote in 1818, but from at least 1845 they had been able to find positions in the civil service.[19] Their advancement, however slow, would have given them hope that one day they would enter political life on terms of full equality with white men. The establishment of Crown Colony government was a severe setback to these aspirations.

In denying islanders the vote, the immediacy of the relationship between government and governed was also removed. This fostered an indifference to the state or colonial authority that continued into the next century and, arguably, exists today.

In 1871, seeking to cut administrative costs and improve efficiency, the British combined the Leeward Islands of Montserrat, Antigua, St. Kitts, Dominica, Anguilla, Nevis, and the Virgin Islands into a single federal colony. The move meant even less government for the Virgin Islands, which had already begun the process of combining government posts. In 1870, the Health Officer was not only the Surgeon and Public Vaccinator but also the Assistant Judge of the General Court. By 1896, the Commissioner was at once the Medical Officer, Postmaster, Magistrate, and Treasurer. This phenomenon not only saved on demands made on the public purse, it helped to concentrate colonial power on the island. The opportunities for the advancement of black men in positions of official authority were thereby greatly reduced, whereas for women they continued to be nonexistent.

Black men were only reluctantly invited to join the Legislative Council. In 1898, an internal memo between the secretary of state for colonial affairs and the governor of the Leeward Islands records official dissatisfaction with the necessity of having to appoint two blacks as unofficial members of the Virgin Islands Legislative Council. "It's rather a farce to have to appoint [F. A. Pickering] and Mr. Smith to get an official majority but if we are to maintain this form of a Legislative Council I suppose we must accept them as the best official members available," wrote the Leeward Islands Governor.[20] This grudging acceptance is particularly remarkable since by that time Pickering had not only served as the territory's Inspector of Police, Registrar of Births, Marriages, and Deaths, and President's Clerk but also acted as president for at least three years prior. By this time there were approximately 3,689 blacks, 1,546 people of mixed blood, and 52 whites in the territory.

At the beginning of the twentieth century, the territory's political development had regressed still further. Administrative power resided entirely in the hands of the commissioner, with a small, advisory executive council providing nominal representation.

Political power was thus concentrated in the hands of a federally appointed colonial officer to the exclusion of the masses of black people. It may be argued that by excluding both men and women so effectively from power, this era of colonial politics had the effect of serving as an equalizer: Virgin Islanders would have come to see the public sphere of political action primarily as the domain of whites. The possibility of blacks' participation would have been seen to rest, once again, on racial rather than sexual distinctions. However, the few blacks allowed involvement in the affairs of the colony were men. Neither would it have escaped notice that only two of the officers of the civil establishment were women and that these were always nurses, among the lowest paid of the civil servants. The franchise was lost to both men and women alike, but men could be jurors and at least a few were allowed to hold significant public office. The equality under the whip black men and women experienced in the fields during slavery was slowly being eroded. The work of missionaries in post-abolition Virgin Island society eroded it still further.

MISSIONARIES IN POST-ABOLITION VIRGIN ISLANDS

Colonial officials and other observers placed much faith in the civilizing effect of both missionaries and white society. A decade prior to emancipation, Porter had issued a dire warning. Without moral and religious instruction, he said, "emancipation would prove a curse instead of a blessing to the poor people themselves and total loss of property if not of life must be the inevitable result to the white and free coloured inhabitants of all the West India colonies." His sentiments were echoed by Secretary of State for the Colonies Lord Lloyd, who wrote in 1840 that "if a healthy society is to be built up in the [West Indian] islands then it must be built up on the foundations of Christian religion and Christian ethics."

The abandonment of the Virgin Islands by whites in the second half of the nineteenth century proved problematic for these aims. The minutes of the Legislative Council in 1863 are revealing: "In former days when the estates were yet held in comparatively few hands the house of every resident gentleman . . . was a centre of civilisation from which radiated a kind of education which at least preserved the labouring classes from sinking into barbarism." President James R. Longden lamented that "a generation is growing up uninfluenced by the daily spectacle of any higher civilisation than their own." He argued that although "the colony is utterly valueless," continued British expenditure was justified by the fact that "the controlling influence of an English gentleman, supported by the English government, is absolutely necessary, at least until the negroes are sufficiently educated to be capable of self-government."[21] (That the British made little effort to provide education of the standard that would prepare Virgin Islanders for self-government will be discussed further on.)

Of course the higher, Christian civilization referred to by Porter, Lloyd, and others was a patriarchal European one. Despite the missionaries' best efforts, however, the paucity of their number and of the number of whites overall meant a somewhat imperfect adoption of patriarchal norms by the former slaves and their descendants.

Abolition came on the eve of the Victorian era, in which, despite the assumption of the throne by a woman, "the wife was in no sense her husband's equal, but, in addition to serving as household manager and social arbiter, she was most obviously and significantly the mother of his children."[22] Women's involvement in waged labor was seen not only as a threat to man's dominion inside the home but also as a threat *outside* the home, to his abilities as breadwinner. Women who worked were thus undermining the very foundation of European civilization as articulated by philosophers and others through the centuries. If male labor was seen as "the motive force of civilization," then women who worked outside the home threatened the male earning power on which civilization was seen to rest.

As Catherine Hall charges, many abolitionists saw emancipation as the period when black women would become like the white women "of the English middle-class imagination, occupying their small but satisfying sphere, married and living in regular households."[23] But the ambitions of the missionaries were initially frustrated by economic conditions in the colony. Post-abolition Virgin Islands saw the migration of hundreds of workers to other islands. Women's labor was needed on what estates remained and, in fact, planters may then have been even more dependent on it. The status quo was therefore allowed to continue. A visitor in 1840 reported seeing "a large number of negroes, male and female," engaged in holeing.

It was only with the disappearance of the estate system that Virgin Islands women began to conform to the traditional expectations of European women. In 1865, President Longden wrote that he attributed the "comparative healthiness of the infant population . . . to the fact that the mothers are almost always employed about their own houses and grounds, and do not have to leave their houses and children to work upon estates."[24] Economic conditions were forcing a gradual assimilation of patriarchal values, but it should be noted that the work women were doing was still predominantly agricultural in nature.

The influence of the Methodists grew after emancipation. A visitor to the West Indies in the 1840s declared that "under the banner of liberty the churches and meeting houses have been enlarged and multiplied, the attendance has become regular and devout." Evidence exists to bear this out. The Blue Book of 1850 records that "the Wesleyans have seven chapels and two houses are used as preaching places, the number generally attending their services are 3,550." That may have been a particularly good year, however, for President Longden's 1864 report claims only 1,660 members for the Methodists and not more than 1,000 for the Anglicans. Whether this decrease can be attributed to the territory's declining fortunes or to other causes is a matter for speculation.[25]

Joan French argues that "in the transition from slavery to emancipation . . . women lost more than men. One of the reasons was that from the final decades of slavery, European nuclear-style marriages was promoted . . . as a way of encouraging population growth."

As has been suggested, this process suffered some setbacks in the Virgin Islands. In 1843, the Stipendiary Magistrate boasted that "concubinage, formerly so general, is now looked upon as sinful and disgraceful and marriage is encouraged and respected. During the last twelve months there have been 101 marriages." Twenty years later, however, marriages had dropped to twenty-nine, rising only to thirty-seven in 1864. The Methodist Church was far more successful at marrying off its converts than was the Church of England. In 1843 the Wesleyans performed eighty-three marriages, but the established church managed only eighteen. In 1850, the Wesleyans conducted thirty-four marriages, but the Church of England racked up only two.

The economic decline certainly may have had an impact on marital and personal relationships. The disinterest in marriage may have owed something to the belief that "a wife . . . should not be expected to work for wages outside the family," as Simey charges, and if so, would certainly indicate a victory for patriarchal practices. The scarcity of employment, the low wages available, and the high rate of male migration meant that finding a man to support them while they sat idle was difficult, if not undesirable for Virgin Islands women. Poor economic conditions may also have meant that many simply could not afford the cost of a wedding. According to one writer, the missionaries demanded "prohibitive fees for officiating" at weddings. Since weddings, at least on Tortola, were weeklong events to which whole communities were invited, their expense may certainly have influenced their frequency. In 1844, marriage expenses for the daughter of a laborer totaled 115 dollars, including 43 dollars for the dress and 27 dollars for the bride cake.[26]

Factors such as the heightened role of the state in child welfare may have played equally important roles in the falling marriage rate. President Longden reported in 1865 that "provision had been made for the first time for compelling the fathers of illegitimate children, relieved at the public expense, to repay the amount of such relief into the Treasury." This was crucial since rates of illegitimacy continued high. "Nearly 42% of the births last year [1864] were illegitimate ... chastity is certainly not a virtue of the West Indian negroes, but their very indifference to it does away with the misery and wretchedness that generally attend the birth of illegitimate children in England. As there is no great shame attached to the birth of illegitimate children there is no temptation to conceal it."[27]

Although two Virgin Gorda women, Margaret Vanterpool and Lucretia Vanterpool, were hanged on 29 March 1858 for causing the death of Margaret's infant child, it is unclear that they did so from motives of shame.

That illegitimacy was viewed with no great censure would have removed any immediate imperative to get married.

Of course until the Married Women's Property Act was passed in Britain on 1 July 1887 and became law in the colony, married women were not considered capable of acquiring, holding, and disposing property. In fact, upon marriage all of the woman's property was deemed to belong to her husband. Virgin Islands women who had become landowners through dint of their thrift and hard work could well have been loath to see their property come under their husband's ownership.

If the missionaries failed or had only mixed success in promoting marriage and reducing illegitimacy, their successes in curbing cultural customs were also mixed. Up to 1834, visitors were still recording the existence of "the more harmless pageant of Jonkanoo with its little emblem of Noah's Ark" that were accompanied by "gamboys (Eboe drums), Shaky Shakers and Kitty Katies." But references to these customs petered out, and by the beginning of the next century, Junkanoo, a masquerade festival (or John Canoe as it is sometimes known), was said to be unknown in the Virgin Islands.

Several laws were passed to aid in the demise of the former slaves cultural practices. In 1847, the Virgin Islands legislature debated a bill prohibiting "any person [from] playing upon any kind of instrument any other than sacred music" on Sunday. In 1866, an ordinance was passed prohibiting "disorderly houses and other places in the town" that keep up an "incessant drumming" and in which "doubtless, mischievous plots are frequently planned."

A report written almost twenty years later gives us another clue about the clandestine continuation of certain cultural practices. "It is hoped to put a stop to the practise of obeah—an African superstition that is generally practised and believed in by the lower orders of the people," wrote President Arthur Rumbold in 1866, decades after Porter had triumphantly declared obeah's extinction. These practices, the legacy of Virgin Islanders' African ancestry, remained outside the parameters of influence exercised by the missionaries. For this reason it may be supposed that European patriarchal conventions had little effect and that, in these and perhaps other cultural practices, women retained the influential role they had enjoyed during slavery.

NOTES

1. "An Act to Repeal the Act Entitled 'An Act to Extend His Majesty's Free Coloured and Free Black Subjects of the Virgin Islands Qualified in the Manner Hereinafter Mentioned All the Rights, Privileges and Immunities Which Are Now Held and Enjoyed by Others of His Majesty's Subjects,'" 6 September 1831. *CO 315/8.*

2. Although some, like the Nottinghams, manumitted their slaves before leaving, many took their slaves with them to other islands where slavery had not been abolished. An account is given of a Mrs. Threlfal who, in the period just before abolition persuaded some of her workers to go to St. John and put them to work there as slaves. President H. Drummond Hay to Governor Cunningham, 31 January 1846. *CO 239/80.*

3. Report of the Stipendiary Magistrate, 21 December 1845. *CO 239/80.* Stipendiary magistrates were officials tasked with helping to ease black people's transition from slavery to freedom.

4. Drummond Hay was president at the time. He served from 1839 to 1851. Norwell Harrigan and Pearl Varlack, *The Virgin Islands Story* (Essex: Caribbean Universities Press in association with Bowker Publishing, 1975), appx. III.

5. Governor Cunningham to Earl Grey, 25 August 1846. *CO 239/81.*

6. The emancipation of slaves in the Danish islands had given rise to "a desire on the part of the planters there to obtain labour from this island [Tortola] for St. Croix." Report of the Stipendiary Magistrate, 31 December 1848. *CO 243/10.*

7. Trash was the dried leaves of the sugarcane, which was used, among other things, as roofing material.

8. Enclosure in Stipendiary Magistrate's Report, 30 June 1847. *CO 243/10.*

9. The colonial officer with immediate responsibility for the Virgin Islands has been known by various terms, including "president," "commissioner," "administrator," and "governor" (the latest appellation). The names corresponded to changed duties and responsibilities.

10. Report by George Porter, colonial secretary, 13 August 1853. *CO 239/95.*

11. President Lt. Col. Chads to Governor Mackintosh, 2 August 1853. *CO 239/95.*

12. According to St. Thomas's *Tidende,* which carried an account of the trial of at least two rioters, Henry Haragan and Pompey Turnbull, "sentence of death was

passed upon 3 and recorded against 4, guilty of the capital offence." *Tidende*, 21 December 1853, p. 3. A number of others were imprisoned for up to six months.

13. In 1841 there were only four. Report of Stipendiary Magistrate, 3 December 1841. *CO 239/66*.

14. Minutes of the Board of Privy Council, 14 October 1846. *CO 239/81*.

15. Governor Hamilton to Lord Buliver, 10 July 1858. *CO 314/6*.

16. President Thomas Price to Governor Hamilton, 29 March 1858. *CO 314/6*. Price recommended rotating officials among the Leeward Islands, a move he felt would improve efficiency and remove corruption.

17. Letter from President Rumbold to Governor Pine, 1 June, 1866. *CO 314/16*. By the end of that year, Rumbold had persuaded Pine to conclude that "it may . . . be the case in the Virgin Islands . . . that the retention of the elective franchise tends to engender strife, falsehood and corruption." Pine to Rumbold, 29 December 1866. *CO 314/16*.

18. Rumbold to Pine, 7 January 1867. *CO 314/17*.

19. In 1845, Charles Stoutt, a native, was promoted in the postal service. Report of the Stipendiary Magistrate, 16 December 1845. *CO 239/80*. Dookhan reports that of the sixteen offices held by coloreds in 1848, only one was held by a Virgin Islander, a situation that may have aggravated feelings of powerlessness and rage among native blacks. Dookhan, p. 154. The ascendance of coloreds in the civil service would have heightened any perception by blacks of being deliberately marginalized. The memory of slavery when coloreds were often set apart and favored probably rankled, leading to the desire to "destroy whites and coloreds."

20. Memo from Governor of the Leeward Islands to Secretary of State for Colonial Affairs, 3 February 1898. *CO 152/229*.

21. Longden to Governor Pine, 23 May 1866. *CO 314/16*.

22. Walter L. Arnstein, *Britain Yesterday and Today: 1830 to the Present*, vol. 4 (London: D. C. Heath, 1992), p. 82.

23. Catherine Hall, "Gender Politics and Imperial Politics: Rethinking the Histories of Empire," in *Engendering History: Caribbean Women in Historical Perspective*, ed. Verene Shepherd, Bridget Brereton, and Barbara Bailey (Kingston: Ian Randle Publishers, 1995), pp. 53–54.

24. Report accompanying Blue Book, 1865. *CO 234/20*.

25. Patterson quotes a contemporary writer who suggested that the enthusiastic religious devotion of the slaves during and immediately after emancipation was due to their "zest for freedom and a token of gratitude to the preachers." Orlando Patterson, *The Sociology of Slavery: An Analysis of the Origins, Development and Structure of Negro Slave Society in Jamaica* (Rutherford: Fairleigh Dickinson University Press, 1969), p. 215.

26. Stipendiary Magistrate's Report, 31 December 1844. *CO 239/73*.

27. President Longden to Governor of the Leeward Islands, 1865. *CO 234/20*.

CHAPTER 4

New Challenges

WOMEN IN POST-ABOLITION SOCIETY AND ECONOMY

In 1856, "Jane Carney was stripped naked by several young men including sons of Charles Lloyd, tarred and feathered and made to walk the streets naked."[1] The "legitimate and illegitimate" sons of Charles Lloyd disapproved of Carney's impending marriage to their father and used this public humiliation as a warning or punishment for her temerity. According to President Thomas Price, the woman was alleged to have been a "prostitute of the lowest order, unfaithful even since her maintenance in Mr. Lloyd's house." We are not told Carney's race, but the incident, like those mentioned in chapter 1, serves to illustrate the vulnerability of all women to physical violence. White women obviously did not face racial oppression, but as women, they too were considered lesser beings. (This Charles Lloyd was the same one who had once represented free black men and who had been elected Speaker of the House.)

Caribbean plantation society was brutal and horrific; it validated the oppression of one race by another. Within that context black women faced a situation of tripled jeopardies. Enslaved, they were denigrated not only for their *race* but for their *sex*. Maligned as Jezebels but, ironically, defeminized as the physical equals of their men, black women's labor capacity as well as their bodies had been placed at the disposal of white men. The mythology that arose about black women's promiscuity was designed to rationalize those aspects of slavery that denied them participation in European standards of feminine decency. Their half-clothed state was thus seen as evidence of licentiousness, not as the result of planters' policies about clothing distribution. Their nakedness, in turn, served to justify planters' lusts and appeared to substantiate the Jezebel stereotype. As it is now for modern-day prostitutes in many countries, nineteenth-century law in the Virgin Islands did not recognize that a black woman could be raped. Like the prostitutes of today, black women were considered sexually available to any man; it was inconceivable that they could have the power to say no. The black woman's productive and reproductive capacities were subjugated to the demands of white male–dominated plantation society. She was the harlot who was expected to work like a man while producing children to increase her owner's profit margin. So pervasive was this mythology that some black men bought into it. They began to see black women as white men saw them and wished them to be seen. Removed by emancipation from the sexual domination of white men, black women sought ways to protect themselves from black men.

At a Methodist Quarterly Meeting in 1835, it was agreed that "no all-night prayer meetings would be permitted on Methodist Church premises" since this led to parents leaving "their daughters unprotected all night."[2] But this measure, even if enforced, did not seem to help. Five years later, rape was still a big problem. The chief justice noted that prosecutions for rape had "certainly been more frequent of late." He attributed this to "the great increase of ... moral feeling and self-respect amongst our labouring classes, so that offences which they formerly viewed with but too little indignation and horror now ... causes resort to our laws for protection." [3] More likely the actual number of rapes had not increased; emancipated black women were now simply taking ownership of their bodies in a way they could not before. Now free, black women may naturally have assumed that the state would finally offer them the same protection it extended to white women. This was not the case. They in fact received very little support from the colonial administration.

In 1840, the ten-year-old niece of the black overseer on Appleby Day Estate was raped by Pero, a laborer, who confessed to a constable and the estate manager. The child was seen by a doctor, who testified as to the presence of inflammation and enlargement of the vagina. He, however, ended up concluding that "penetration of a finger might have produced the same effect." Though he also saw a discharge, he further testified that it could have been caused by disease. Pero was convicted but recommended for a free pardon since the only evidence against him was his confession. President H. Drummond Hay, Governor MacPhail from Antigua, the attorney general and the private secretary all consented to the granting of the pardon.

During slavery black women had been the sexual prey of choice for white men. An entire body of beliefs had arisen asserting black women's supposedly rampant sexuality. Black women's bodies were at the disposal of white men and disposable. A black girl's charges of sexual assault, even if against a black man, could hope to elicit little sympathy from white men. The fact that Pero had actually confessed to the crime should at least have removed the doctor's doubts about the actual form of penetration and the cause of the discharge. In fact, the doctor's conclusions suggest his contempt for black women and girls. Despite the general backwardness of medical standards at the time, the doctor should have known that ten-year-old girls are not prone to vaginal diseases unless they have had sexual intercourse.

Economically, the territory's fortunes declined and so did wages. By 1859, one-third of the Virgin Islands population consisted of children under ten and people over sixty. Hundreds of Virgin Islanders, both men and women, left to seek work in the Danish islands.[4] There, women found ready employment as seamstresses, washers, house servants, coal carriers, sellers, ground laborers, housekeepers, and cake makers. Most were in their twenties and thirties. Some were in their teens. Sara Digby, 14, was employed as a servant in 1870, as were Mary Harrigan, 19, and her sister, Susanna Harrigan, 16. A few were even younger. Rosanna Thodman, 11, was registered in the 1870 census as a washer; Marian Linch, 7, was a servant and Margret Hodge, 11, was a domestic. The oral tradition holds that children, both girls and boys, were sent to St. Thomas to attend school and generally make a better life for themselves. The evidence suggests that, instead, some were put to work by the families to whom they were sent, and sometimes by their own parents.

For the adult women who chose to go to the Danish islands to find work, their decision represented a new physical autonomy. People who had once been slaves were now able to make choices about what to do with their lives. Such personal freedom must have been exhilarating. But not everyone was happy about the choices people were making. Governor Hamilton wrote disapprovingly about the behavior of some Virgin Islanders in St. Thomas. According to him, "the President reported the conduct of the black population as orderly in general; although many young people of both sexes are corrupted by the licentious habits prevailing at the coaling station of St. Thomas to which they resort for employment."

Previous presidents had not expressed much concern about the licentious habits prevailing in and encouraged by plantation society. It is possible to surmise that the president, like other white Virgin Islanders of the time, would have preferred black Virgin Islanders to stay in the territory. Their migration was a nail in the coffin of large-scale agriculture. More and more able-bodied laborers working for better wages in other islands meant fewer and fewer laborers to work on what sugar estates remained. But Virgin Islanders were seeking improved lives for themselves and their children. They could not create these lives in the territory, not even on Tortola, which was the biggest and most prosperous island. Even Road Town, which had the highest concentration of free blacks during slavery, could not, decades after emancipation, boast a sizeable middle class.

The greater majority of Virgin Islands women therefore had to work and continued to do so in the field, though not on the estates. They could not afford the indolent life of European women in the Caribbean. Instead, they planted and harvested crops of yams, tannias, cassava, toulama and other ground provisions, which they then sold at the weekly market or around the territory. Many also burnt charcoal, which was either sold locally or exported to St. Thomas.

Black women's labor during their enslavement rebutted the image of the weak, frail, and subservient woman dependent on her man for sustenance. Now that they were emancipated, their industry would become the foundation on which the survival of their families depended. In 1857, the president reported that "the patches of garden culture where almost every description of tropical vegetable may be seen in tolerable luxuriance, even at the highest points of our lofty hills, prove satisfactorily that wherever the Negro has, by the absolute purchase of land, obtained an interest in its productiveness, that productiveness is in fair development."

Seven years later the prospect of land ownership became real for hundreds more. After the West Indies Encumbered Estates Act was passed in 1864, more than 780 acres were sold for a total of £979. It is impossible to say just how many women were among those buying land. Given their financial self-sufficiency and enterprising spirit, it is probably safe to assume that many saw land ownership as the good investment opportunity it was. President Longden reported in 1865 that not only is "the greater part of the soil owned by negroes" but "one in every ten is a freeholder and one in every six is possessed of sufficient property to be directly taxed." In that year there were 585 freeholders and 1,119 people paying direct taxes.

Although the history of large-scale plantations in the post-emancipation era is largely one of failure, the former slaves and their descendants did grow "small patches" of sugarcane or cotton. Along with ground provisions and the successful breeding of livestock such as horned cattle and goats, these "small patches" earned many families a living. But not everybody saw this as a triumph.

In these islands "we are face to face with the problem of governing a colony composed almost exclusively of petty negro proprietors . . . every man cultivates his own land and carries his own produce for sale to St. Thomas," President Longden complained in 1866.[5] What he may have seen as a problem, however, was, in reality, evidence of personal independence and self-reliance. These qualities have ensured that although the territory remains a colony to this day, its people have attained a measure of individual autonomy and affluence uncommon in many of the other islands where plantation economies continued to flourish and the factors of large population and size added their dynamics.

Accustomed to hard work and to making ends meet, black women may even have had a better time of it following emancipation than their former mistresses. Having relied on the income gained from hiring out their slaves and/or apprentices or from employing them as hucksters or on such land as they possessed, white women found themselves economically bereft at the end of slavery. Even the widows of public servants did not fare well. Commenting on the Virgin Islands, the Leeward Islands governor wrote that there is "some evidence that widows of public servants have been left penniless upon death of their husbands in office."[6] In a small island economy of peasant proprietors, the incorporated wives of colonial officials, women whose status derived from their husbands, had made little or no space for themselves.[7] Constrained by the stereotypes to which they had submitted, these white women found it difficult to step off their pedestals and into the muddy fields of commerce and agriculture.

During slavery, matrons at the jail had been white women, usually the wives of prison administrators or other colonial officials. Women continued to fill these positions, but it is difficult to say whether white women continued to dominate. Between 1840 and the turn of the century several women held the post of matron at the jail, the infirmary, or the poorhouse. Matrons after 1834 included Amelia Austin, Mary Sydraite, and Ellen Dyer. The latter was appointed matron of the jail in 1843, was paid an annual salary of £25, and was then the only woman on the public payroll. Like the matrons before her, Dyer lived in the prison. After she vacated the post, the matron of the jail began to be paid less and less. Whether this was because black women were now being appointed to these positions or because the economy had gone into a steep decline is difficult to say. Penelope Crawford, who also lived in the jail in the 1870s, made only £20 per year. Ann Polina Pickering, who was matron of the jail in the 1880s, made even less—£15 per year. Meanwhile, the matron of the infirmary, a position held by Rebecca Pickering in the 1870s, made £15 annually. It is unclear whether the infirmary also served as the poorhouse, but in the 1870s, Catherine Arundel served as matron of the poorhouse and received an annual salary of £15. Elizabeth Ann Joseph succeeded her to the post in the 1880s at the same salary. Except for the matrons, women were excluded from the civil establishment.

Meanwhile, the difference in the treatment of female prisoners as opposed to male meant that by 1879, the separation of the sexes was complete—"Males being entirely under the turnkey and females under the Matron."[8] Male prisoners were often employed outside the prison, marking and repairing Road Town's single street and cleaning public places. Female prisoners, on the other hand, were never employed outside. Instead they were required to "break stones, wash and mend the prison clothes, and keep the interior of the prison clean." Except for the first duty, it is clear that women's work within the prison reflected the gender conventions of the time.

Evidence exists to suggest that black and colored women continued to plunge into commercial enterprises. During his visit to the territory immediately after emancipation, Joseph John Gurney reports staying at a tavern for travelers owned by a "coloured old lady," Mrs. McCleverty. And huckstering thrived.

In 1843, the Stipendiary Magistrate wrote that "there are small huckstering shops in every part of this colony and all classes of the community are more or less engaged in retail dealings. Hucksters are constantly to be seen travelling about the country and passing from plantation to plantation with trays of goods which are readily and profitably disposed of to the Negroes."[9] The hucksters sold everything from printed muslin to salted provisions to cornmeal.

Government acknowledged the importance of huckstering to the internal economy with an act requiring hucksters to obtain a license. Passed 28 April 1859, the act stipulated that "any person having obtained a huckster's license . . . shall be authorized to carry about within the Virgin Islands in Baskets, Boxes, Trunks, Trays or other conveyances Goods, Wares and Merchandise for sale by wholesale and retail." The government clearly hoped to profit off the enterprise of black women. President George Porter reported in 1864 that "shops of all kinds, hucksters and pedlars are taxed at rates ranging from £2.8 to £20 a year."[10]

In a society as close to and dependent on the sea as the Virgin Islands, it is not unreasonable to expect women also to have been involved in fishing, and this was indeed the case. A letter from President Porter to Governor Hill in 1868 records the existence of at least two female boat owners—a Mrs. Callwood of Thatch Island and a Johanna Smith of Peter Island. As these women were resident on the outer islands, their boats provided independence of movement, but it is unlikely that they would have owned boats that were not also put to commercial use.

Though historians now write of the Virgin Islands as barely subsisting before the introduction of the hotel industry in the 1960s, the fact is that an agrarian-based economy did flourish in these islands. Women were a vibrant part of this economy. The census of 1891 records the existence of 212 laundresses and washers, 104 female domestics, 459 agricultural laborers, 12 bakers, 2 hotel keepers, 26 peddlers, and 254 seamstresses.[11] Men did not participate in several of these business sectors (laundering and washing, hotel keeping, peddling, and sowing) and were underrepresented in others (there was only one male baker), indicating the hardening of a division of labor based on gender. More importantly, though, this census testified to women's pervasive participation in the waged labor force of the time. The difference between these women and the working women of today is, of course, the nature of the work in which women were involved. As bakers and seamstresses, for instance, women worked within their own homes. This contributed to local adoption of the patriarchal myth of the stay-at-home mother, a misunderstanding of women's real historical role within the Virgin Islands economy.

Beside their business undertakings, women continued to serve their communities as midwives or schoolteachers. As the former they earned very little in the way of hard currency, and it is unlikely that the latter earned much either. In 1903, the Executive Council minutes record the existence of at least two midwives, Jane Ann O'Neal and Susanna Varlack. At that time the doctor charged £2 per visit, so it is likely that midwives such as these women earned substantially less.

There is not much written evidence of the sterling service midwives performed in the territory. But local dependence on them must have been high, given the frequent lack of a doctor and the distances he had to travel to get to those who needed him.[12] Midwives would probably have been found in almost every community. The census of 1891 records the existence of eight. The status they enjoyed during slavery would have remained much the same.

EDUCATION AND WOMEN

Information about the number of women teachers and the number of pupils is more readily available and suggests that education may have been seen as more beneficial to girls than boys.[13]

In 1841, the Stipendiary Magistrate reported that "male teachers seem to have been generally preferred in the schools" for their ability to enforce corporal punishment. But whatever the preference of parents, the lead women had taken in offering education continued. Mention is made in the House of Commons Parliamentary Papers of an attempt by two women to open a school in Anegada in 1837.[14] The school closed soon after for want of funds, but "dame schools," as they were called, sprang up all over the colony. In 1844, the Stipendiary Magistrate reported that "a dame school has recently been established at Jost Van Dyke." By 1845, seven of the ten day schools run by the Church of England in the Virgin Islands were being run by women. Four of the seven were "the daughters of Africans at Kingstown and who were themselves taught at the Kingstown school." Other schools were located at Road Town, Sea Cows Bay, Windy Hill, Mount Healthy, Salt Island, Virgin Gorda, Anegada, and Jost Van Dyke. Five years later the Blue Book of 1850 reported that there were seven schools and that women taught at five of them.

Although the majority of people attended the Wesleyan Methodist Church, the Church of England was the definite leader in offering some form of education to the freed slaves and their descendants. The reports of the Stipendiary Magistrate for the half year ending 31 December 1845 records that approximately 400 children attended the day schools established by the Church of England, whereas only 134 attended the Wesleyan schools.

Women-run schools included Eliza Coakley's at West End, which was operational in the 1850s, Miss Thomas's at East End, which was operational in the 1860s, and Amelia Harrigan's at Peter Island, which was functional in the 1870s. Unfortunately, we know little about these pioneering women besides their names.

Initially, the number of girls and boys attending the various schools was fairly equal.[15] In 1843, the number of boys attending the Church of England's day schools stood at 269, and the number of girls was 275.[16] In 1848, the numbers were still fairly equal, with 146 boys and 155 girls attending those schools. Seventy-seven boys and 99 girls attended the Wesleyan schools. By 1860, however, the gap was wider. The Road Town Church of England school, run by Eliza Dyer, reported the attendance of 35 females as opposed to 21 males, whereas the Kingstown school, run by Catherine Chalwell, reported 36 females and 24 males. The Anegada school run by Mrs. Farrington had 30 males and 40 females. By this time the economy was in serious decline, and it is conceivable that boys were taking the place of absent migrant fathers in the fields. Some may even have been migrating themselves.

The gender gap for adults was even wider. A report on instruction in reading given at Wesleyan Sunday schools for adults puts female attendance in Road Town at 26 and male at 10. In Jost Van Dyke 12 men and 20 women attended the Sunday school.

Like the day schools, Sunday schools around the territory recorded higher female attendance than male, the biggest difference being in Road Town, which had 77 males as opposed to 140 females. In 1861, the Wesleyan school at Road Town recorded attendance by 45 males and 138 females.

Given the fluctuating and uneven nature of education before the Education Act of 1925 was introduced, it is difficult to make a certain analysis of the figures. One could, however, speculate that the territory's drop in fortunes may have led to a feeling of education's irrelevance for boys, who could easily find agricultural or other work elsewhere. Shrinking government meant shrinking opportunities for Virgin Islanders to join the civil service, where their education would have been useful. In addition, the reliance on agriculture combined with the missionaries' position on the inappropriateness of agricultural work for girls might have demanded the presence of boys in the fields.

Sending girls to school could also have been seen as a way of keeping them out of trouble and of educating them in such ladylike skills as needlework. In reality, it gave them an educational head start and provided them with important female role models. In fact, teaching gave women the most effective means of entering public life. This lesson would not have been lost on girls or, indeed, on the community.

The education offered at day schools, however, was limited. It was of the "most elementary kind" designed simply to "diminish crime and to train up a race of industrious God-fearing colonists."[17]

Sunday school aims were similar. Students were expected to learn "their duty to God, to their parents and to their superiors."[18] This largely meant that students received an education that heavily emphasized religion. Repetition of the catechism and reading and spelling from the Psalms and the Old Testament took up most, if not all, of the school day. There was one difference, however. In addition to those classes already mentioned, boys learned writing and basic arithmetic. This was not so for girls. Education was perceived as being of little use for them unless it prepared them for their feminine tasks, so their extra class was plain needlework. Until the passage of the Education Act in 1925, the curriculum did not change much. Education was in the hands of the church, and the colonial administration in the person of the president saw little need for improvement.

Instead, President Longden blamed the "indifference of many of the parents" for the failures of an education system that he deemed "sufficient for the wants of the population." But Longden's confidence in the educational status quo was not shared by the inspector general of schools, who made regular visits to the territory from his base on Antigua. In 1875, none of the ten schools passed the inspector general's examination, and four were struck off his list for exceptional aid. Two years later the situation improved slightly. Of the nine schools examined, one passed, and none was struck off the list.

The inspector found much to dissatisfy him. "Schools are in remote places not under constant supervision . . . [and are] taught by under-paid and untrained teachers," he wrote. Unlike Longden, however, he found that parents were "fully alive to the great advantages of education." Unfortunately, this did not prevent the territory from holding the record for lowest general attendance out of the six islands inspected.[19] The inferior education offered in the territory was a symptom of its deliberate underdevelopment. Female teachers' low wages were a sign of this underdevelopment and pointed to women's subordinate status within Virgin Islands society. In 1881, only one female teacher, Mrs. Creque in Anegada, made more than £15 per year. Mrs. Harrigan on Peter Island made £10, Mrs. Potter, the sewing mistress on Anegada, made £2.10s, Miss Haddock on Jost Van Dyke made £12.10s, and Miss Penn in East End made £15. In comparison, Mr. Haddock (Miss Haddock's father), who taught in Road Town, made £30, and Mr. Harrigan, who taught in West End, made £20. The unequal pay reflected the attitudes of the times, which determined that men needed to be paid more since they were supposed to be the breadwinners for their families. The adoption of European patriarchal ideology did not bow to local conditions.

As we have seen in this chapter, many men (as well as some women) emigrated in search of better conditions, leaving women to manage the farms and families left behind. The census of 1891 reported that "in each of the islands the females preponderate and although the mortality is greater among the male than the female children the preponderance is mainly due to the emigration of many of the younger men who leave the Colony hoping to better their position."

The post-emancipation era thus saw the economic decline of the Virgin Islands in terms of its worth as a plantation colony. This decline was accompanied by a political deterioration that led to the gradual obliteration of the gains made by black men in the years preceding abolition. Although it may be concluded that the territory's poverty as a colony made it valueless to the Empire (and certainly, the Empire itself appeared to come to that conclusion), the freedom gained by the slaves on 1 August 1834 was made more real and more immediate by the territory's neglect. In other words, the very declaration by colonial officials of the Virgin Islands's worthlessness ensured a prolonged period in which the newly freed slaves were left alone by the authorities to develop the virtues of self-reliance and personal autonomy.

In 1888, it was said of Virgin Islanders that "the greater number of them own some small portion of land and stock; they work for themselves, when and as they please, and what their labour produces is their own. . . . They are not rich, but are in most cases far removed from a condition of poverty . . . it's only amongst the townspeople who own no land and in case of old age or desertion, that real harsh poverty is present."[20]

It could be argued that without the vote and without political participation, Virgin Islanders were kept in a state of political infancy, almost as Rousseau's "noble savages," but the very distance of the state fostered an indifference that allowed Virgin Islanders to forge their own individual destinies.

In colonial societies the colonial state is very present and is reflected everywhere in laws, institutions, social policy, and so on. But for the Virgin Islands, removed by a distance of many miles from the seat of real colonial authority in Antigua, the state was not at all an ever-present reality. In fact, it existed almost solely in the presence of the commissioner, whom Virgin Islanders, particularly those in the country and sister islands, rarely saw. Ignored for the most part by Great Britain and the neighboring English colonies, Virgin Islanders concentrated on family, community, and land ownership. Decades of isolation bred an insularity among the people in which family came first and community second. Hemmed in by hills, these communities existed as isolated islands within islands. This sociocultural environment bred a hardy individualism in which many of the strengths and

weaknesses of the Virgin Islander's personality are based. It also fostered a
suspicion of authority that found expression in the demonstrations of the
next century. This heritage of colonialism, neglect, and insularity is at the
foundation of a basic unawareness of politics as a force that can be used to
shape people's lives. It was not until the 1930s and 1940s that islanders, gal-
vanized by events in the rest of the Caribbean, bestirred themselves to seek
enhanced political representation. But the coming of elective government
and the subsequent economic development brought both an increased paternalism on the part of the British Empire and a hardening or solidification
of patriarchal norms.

NOTES

1. Enc. R. H. Dyett to Lt. Governor Eyre, 8 July 1859. *CO 314/7.*
2. Woodie Blackman, *Methodism: 200 Years in the British Virgin Islands* (Bridgetown, Barbados: BVI Methodist Church, 1989), pp. 77–78.
3. Address by Chief Justice to Grand Jury, August 1840. *CO 239/60.*
4. The 1859 census records 258 males and 173 females as temporary absentees, suggesting that these men and women had gone to St. Thomas and elsewhere
to seek employment. Enc. President Porter to Governor Price, 10 February 1859.
CO 314/7.
5. President Longden to Governor Pine, 23 May 1866. *CO 314/16.*
6. Letter from Leeward Islands Governor to Secretary of State for Colonial Affairs. *CO 314/21.* In those years, cotton, livestock, cattle, and charcoal were the territory's main exports. Blue Book, 1865. *CO 234/20.*
7. Wives of colonial administrators particularly "suffered the problems of 'incorporated' status; that is, a wife's own status and position derived nearly entirely
from her husband's place within the hierarchical structure." Margaret Strobel, *European Women and the Second British Empire* (Bloomington: Indiana University
Press, 1991), p. xii.
8. Blue Book, 1879. *CO 317/50.* Some of those who had been imprisoned under
the Vagrancy Act in the immediate post-emancipation period were fugitive slaves
from the nearby Danish islands of St. John and St. Thomas. Stipendiary Magistrate's Report, 31 December 1845. *CO 243/10* and *House of Commons Parliamentary
Papers, 1839*, vol. 37, pp. 1–91. The Danes did not abolish slavery until 1848. In
1877, thirteen fugitives from St. Croix, five of whom were women, were arrested
on Tortola. The Danish government claimed that they were wanted on charges of
arson and murder and sought their extradition, but they were later released. Tele-
gram from President to Governor in Antigua, enc. no. 5 in no. 262, 11 1877. *CO
152/132.*
9. Stipendiary Magistrate's Report, 31 December 1843. *CO 239/74.*
10. President Porter to Governor Hill, 15 January 1864. *CO 314/14.*
11. *Leeward Islands Census with Tabular Statements and Report, 1891* (rpt., Jamaica: University of the West Indies, Trinidad: Central Statistics Office, 1964), table no. 111.
12. According to Dookhan, "the Virgin Islands had never been blessed with an
abundance of doctors even during the more prosperous days of slavery, and by

1850 there was only one." Isaac Dookhan, *A History of the British Virgin Islands, 1672–1970* (Essex: Caribbean Universities Press in association with Bowker Publishing, 1975), p. 179.

13. An attempt to establish a school for the education of white boys in the mid-1840s was unsuccessful because of parents' failure to pay student fees. For more see Dookhan, p. 179, and President Drummond Hay to Governor Cunningham, 16 February 1846. *CO 239/80.*

14. *House of Commons Parliamentary Papers, 1837*, vol. 48, pp. 288–385. This school, like the others, came under the supervision of the male rector or priest.

15. Except for Sunday schools, which in 1843 recorded attendance by 180 males and 251 females. *House of Commons Parliamentary Papers, 1845*, vol. 31, pp. 484–581.

16. Ibid. Day schools received grants from the Colonial Treasury at the rate of five shillings per child. To qualify for the grants, the schools had to have more than twenty pupils, none of whom could be under age five. The grants were not given for children over age twelve.

17. Report by Longden, 1863, encl. from Governor of the Leeward Islands Edward Cardwell to Secretary for Colonial Affairs Hill, 14 March 1864. *CO 314/14.*

18. Price to Hamilton, report accompanying Blue Book, 1858. *CO 314/6.*

19. These included Antigua, Montserrat, St. Kitts, Dominica, and Nevis.

20. *House of Commons Parliamentary Papers, 1888*, vol. 72, pp. 876–975.

CHAPTER 5

Constructing Self

TWENTIETH-CENTURY GOVERNMENT

In 1901, the wholly nominated legislature provided for in 1867 was abolished. The Virgin Islands was left with an Executive Council that hardly met, so that the Commissioner became the sole symbol of colonial authority in the colony.[1] Much of the activity of the colonial authorities around this time was centered on improving the agricultural situation. Efforts were made by the Department of Agriculture to encourage cotton, lime, and sugarcane cultivation. Though these initiatives realized initial success, the advent of World War I, followed by a hurricane in 1916, ended any hopes for some measure of prosperity.

In 1917, the United States bought the neighboring Danish West Indies of St. Thomas, St. John, and St. Croix. The United States Virgin Islands, as the islands became known, then entered a period of growing prosperity that was unmatched by their British neighbors. Instead, the author of a 1942 report suggested that there should be no attempt to introduce "the educational and social framework of American small town industrial and commercial society into these islands" as had been done in the USVI. Clearly, the British were following a conscious policy of underdevelopment. The Annual General Report for the Leeward Islands for the year 1927–28 reveals that although the British spent £83,149 on Antigua that year, they spent only £7,240 on the Virgin Islands. (Montserrat received the next highest allocation at £19,986.)

Neither had the colonial authorities given up on the introduction of European patriarchal norms. French charges that the Moyne Commission of the 1930s "greatly helped" promote the engendering of gender roles that demanded the submission of women to men.[2] The Commission recommended that women be put on equal terms with men with respect to voting and candidacy eligibility. But it also recommended that, "given their special interest" in these areas, women should serve on those boards or authorities that were concerned with education, housing, medical, land settlements, or social welfare schemes.

This recommendation was a double-edged sword; it sought to consign women only to those spheres of interest that were extensions of the domestic sphere, but it also created the space for women's participation in the public arena from which they had long been excluded. And it did this by acknowledging the importance of the knowledge and skills women had developed in the private/domestic sphere so long deemed as having little importance in civil life. Given the territory's underdevelopment, however, years passed before the commission's recommendations finally began to bear fruit in terms of women's participation on public boards and other similar bodies. In the meantime, Virgin Islanders flooded the islands of their more prosperous neighbors, looking for employment.[3] Many endured living conditions that a College of the Virgin Islands report termed "deplorable" so that they could send remunerations home. For decades then, Virgin Islanders' economic survival depended on their near neighbors.[4] Virgin Islanders over on St. Thomas, St. Croix, and St. John were employed in the construction industry and in private households, working as masons, nurses, chambermaids, and so on.

But in the late 1930s the U.S. government began to tighten immigration restrictions.[5] With their escape valves closing or closed, the impoverishment of Virgin Islanders festered more sorely. At that time the only road capable of handling motor vehicles was in Road Town, there was no high school and no airport, and the island's sole doctor made only infrequent trips to the sister islands.

In 1943, 800 men and women signed a petition circulated by the Virgin Islands Welfare Committee (also known as the Civic League) calling for the whole Virgin Islands group to share one nationality—American. The petitioners also recommended a number of programs aimed at effecting the colony's economic improvement. Materially, there was little result to this petition, but the people's frustrations were becoming increasingly politicized. Political discord peaked in 1949, when more than 1,000 people marched through Road Town to protest "a form of government akin to dictatorship." The marchers presented two petitions to Commissioner J.A.C. "Ian" Cruikshank. One asked for his removal from office, and the other demanded the reestablishment of a Legislative Council. The colonial authorities sat up and took notice.

In the following year a committee was appointed by the commissioner to determine what form the new council should take and who should be given the vote. At a meeting in 1950, "leading men from every large village in Tortola" and the sister islands met to discuss the formation of a new constitution. By the end of the meeting they had agreed to attach property and literacy qualifications to the franchise. More significantly, they recommended that only British males over the age of twenty-one should be permitted to vote. Clearly, the territory's leaders wished to use the political turmoil of the forties and early fifties to secure the freedoms and equalities of the polis for educated and propertied men like themselves.

But the Leeward Islands Act No. 1 of 1950 that established the conditions for the constitution of a locally elected membership system in the Virgin Islands did not exclude women from the franchise, as the men who met at the Road Town Methodist Church Hall had recommended. By that year the metropolitan women's movement was well under way. The suffragettes had bent the British government to their will, and women in England were granted the vote in 1918. The colonial authorities could do no less than grant women in the Virgin Islands that right. The suffrage was extended to anyone who had "attained the age of 21, is not a lunatic, is a British subject and has resided in the Presidency for 12 months" prior to elections.

The qualifications for people seeking election were a bit more stringent. The first Virgin Islands constitution, formulated at the behest of the territory's leaders following mass meetings, contained a strong reactionary feature: only men and women with significant property or income could offer themselves for election. Candidates had to "possess a clear income of at least $480. per annum [or] own real property in the Presidency of the value of at least $1,440 [or] occupy land in the Presidency as tenant to another of rental value of at least $240. per annum."

The money women earned from higgling, sewing, and so on was enough to feed their families, but, unlike the money earned by the men who went to Cuba, the Dominican Republic, and farther afield, it was often not enough to purchase property or start big businesses. They would have been particularly affected by these restrictions.[6] Years before, the Moyne Commission had noted that "women can take little part in the administration of the West Indian colonies when they are eligible to exercise the vote on equal terms with men or to stand with them for election . . . the prescribed qualifications are usually such that few women possess the property or income to satisfy them."

The territory's leaders, in their effort to include income and literacy qualifications, had not moved forward with the times. Instead they were attempting to manipulate and use the political ferment to acquire greater power for themselves and to consolidate their leadership position. Conditioned by colonialism and history to accept rule by the few and in the absence of any mass-based nationalist or labor movement that might have tempered the leaders' elitist and exclusionary inclinations, the people kept silent.

The party that was quickly formed consisted of former Executive Council members and protest leaders.[7] The two demonstration leaders from Road Town, I. G. Fonseca and Carlton de Castro, formed the Progressive League, which fielded four candidates. The leaders won the election, as did two independents, Howard R. Penn and C. Brudenell Bruce, a British expatriate. Political power was thus shared initially by the colonial authority and elite Road Town men.

After the 1950 elections, effective legislative power remained in the hands of the Leeward Islands legislature and executive power continued to reside in the hands of the commissioner. The elected representatives of the people had greater status than if they were simply the un-elected, unofficial members of the Executive Council, but they could not overturn the commissioner's decisions.[8] Their chairmanship of committees such as Trade and Production functioned only to "introduce [them] under a non-responsible constitution to the business of government."[9]

When, in 1953, the introduction of the district system and the removal of income and property qualifications forced the arrival of newcomers, politics became characterized by jockeying for position between the "Town Boys" (the United Three, as the remaining members of the Progressive League were known) and the "Country Boys." Former Chief Minister Cyril Romney claimed, in support of the district system, that it "narrowed the distance between decision-makers and the population." But its implications for women were less optimistic; there was no room in the "Boys'" political scrimmage for them.

Fifteen candidates stood for the 1954 elections, but only 41.3 percent of registered voters went to the polls. Still, the agitation of the thirties and forties was finally beginning to bear fruit. Infrastructural and economic development resulted in motorable roads, the expansion of electricity islandwide on Tortola, and the establishment of a Colonial Agricultural Credit Fund. Colonial authorities were quite willing to give the elected members credit for this. "There can be no doubt that the ideas and driving force provided by the elected members has encouraged the initiation of new projects and has given a faster tempo to every form of development," said the Leeward Islands governor.[10]

Problems remained, however. In 1966, Dr. Mary Proudfoot, the constitutional commissioner appointed by the United Kingdom to look into political conditions in the territory, emphasized the "need to improve the relationship between government on the one hand and people on the other." Consequent on that report, a conference was convened in London in 1966 at which it was agreed that under a new constitution, the administrator would be in charge of external affairs, internal security, the public service, and finance. An Executive Council made up of the chief minister, two other ministers, and two ex-officio members (the attorney general and the financial secretary) would be in charge of everything else and set policy. A Legislative Council would consist of the Speaker, two ex-officio members, one nominated member, and seven elected members.

Three parties were formed in response to these changes. They were the United Party (UP), the BVI Democratic Party (DP), and the People's Own Party (POP). In all, seventeen candidates ran for office in 1967. The United Party won most of the seats. Seventy-one percent of the territory's registered 3,655 voters participated in the elections. The high registration (there were 7,920 people in the Virgin Islands in 1961) and voter turnout suggests that political interest ran high. Many must have felt that Virgin Islanders were finally coming into their own, that a political coming of age was being realized.

The roles women played during these years as community leaders and successful business owners built on the foundation laid by previous generations of women. Women enabled not only their own advancement but that of the territory's as well. Their contributions went unremarked, however, and they were not invited to take direct part in the determination of the colony's political future. Through its appointments to the Executive Council and its nominations of representatives to regional and bilateral meetings with London, the colonial authority made it clear that the reins of power, once handed over, would be securely in male hands.

None of the groups invited to meet with the Moyne Commission in 1938 included a woman representative.[11] In fact, though women had a long history of involvement in education, the representatives of the Teacher's Association, which did meet with the commission, were all men. Thirty years later the situation had not improved much. Of the twenty-four people who met with Dr. Mary Proudfoot, only two were women. They were Community Development Officer Eugenie Todman-Smith and Pearl Varlack, headmistress of the primary and post-primary school at Road Town. Masculine colonial authority interacted with Virgin Islands men, who, in marking themselves as present in the colonial polity, simultaneously marked women as absent. Virgin Islands men were thus acting not simply as intermediaries between women and colonial authority but as if Virgin Islands women should be neither seen nor heard.

The Moyne Commission itself had included two white women: Dr. Mary Blacklock, an expert in tropical medicine, and Dame Rachel Crowdy, a social worker. The Proudfoot Report and the report of Carleen McLaughlin, another woman, were influential in determining the future of the colony. But these women were white and foreign. Their appointment by the colonial authorities signaled no overture to Virgin Islands women. The Moyne Commission's report had been ambiguous at best about the role and status of women in the region. Some commission members actually felt that there was no need for immediate universal suffrage. They thought that extending the vote to "wives of registered electors" who themselves met property and income requirements would sufficiently increase the ranks of women voters. In reality, however, this suggestion, if implemented, would have meant a consolidation of class interests. Proudfoot, herself a woman, had no specific comments or suggestions about women.

From the settlement of the colony in the 1700s, white men had assumed the right to define and articulate the colony's needs and wants to the colonial power. When black men assumed the mantle of political power, they too began to participate in the exclusion of women from traditional politics. Only when one of these men was unavailable were women allowed to act as temporary stand-ins (witness Emmogene Creque's appointment to the legislature, which will be discussed later).

In the rush to form political parties occasioned by the granting of the franchise, women were again marginalized. Yet despite their exclusion, women, particularly elite women, found other effective ways of contributing to the fashioning of Virgin Islands society. The public roles they assumed were founded on a range of social activities, including welfare and cultural work. In this way women's public work directly affected the lives of Virgin Islanders while contributing to the development of social policy. But it did so against the odds; several factors militated against women's involvement.

WOMEN IN THE SOCIETY AND IN THE FAMILY

In the absence of modern conveniences during the first half of this century, women continued to lead lives of strenuous toil. They lugged "loads of wash to [nearby] springs or ghuts for cleaning, carried buckets to the house, [and] burned charcoal for cooking and ironing" as well as for sale. Since there was no piped water, ghuts (ravines of flowing water) were the laundries of the day. Women took bundles of clothes to the nearest ghut to be scrubbed, licked, and boiled with soap bush, corn husks, or the roots of either the maiden apple or the peter gum tree. The clothes would then be taken home again, where they were hung on wild pineapple fences to dry. Women also carried water for household purposes from the ghuts back to their homes. *Cottas*, a thick coil of cloth, provided some protection for their heads from the zinc buckets, calabash gourds, or demijohns that they used.

Women's work did not stop at providing water for their families' needs. Leonora Freeman, eighty-five, remembers "going into the pasture, tending to my cattle. . . . We got help from an older man who I asked to set up the coal pit, bush it dirt it and light it." Freeman sold the coal only from her house, but many other women sold coal at the market or sent it to St. Thomas for sale.

Many bartered for what they didn't have. "People from out in the country where I'm from would take provisions to people in East End in exchange for fish because money wasn't prevalent," recalls Ilva Lettsome. The bartering system pointed to the deep personal ties that existed among women in their own communities and between the women of different communities. In effect, women created and used a supportive network that ensured their survival and that of their children. Even women with nothing to barter could count on this network.

Lettsome remembers that the practice was called "hand-in-hand."

Like every Saturday now six of us or four of us would kill some animal like goat, pigs, calves. Then that meat would share around to the neighbours . . . then six or seven of us would be in the ground and we'd send tannias, yams, potatoes, cassava, toulup and toulama to who ain't have. If Mrs. Forbes say, didn't have a cow we'd tell her to send her child and then they would take the flasks and she would get two flasks of milk.[12]

In these ways women contributed not only to each other's well-being but, in fact, to the survival of their communities. Though they may not have known it, their cooperation with each other was a legacy of African traditions in which it is common for members of a clan or tribe to see to each other's welfare.

Women's lives were not all work and no play. They often participated in the musical life of their communities. The history of the Great Britain Band, a band of carolers, makes this clear. Formed by Camelita Greaves around the turn of the century, the leadership of the band was later taken over by Rosanna Helena Smith. A biography of Smith recounts that she was a member of the band for sixty years, leading it in their competitions with other roving bands of carolers.

Special occasions such as weddings also helped families and communities to form and cement ties. One writer describes a typical wedding.

The mother of the bride would set up the reception in her "yard," the area behind her house and would construct a tent made of coconut palms. Family and friends would cook food: everyone would bring something to eat or drink. The bride's mother was responsible for the cakes, tart, and fruit. The groom's family was responsible for the drinks—the men of the groom's family would bring quantities of cane rum for the occasion and the groom's father would bring a bull for the feast, or sometimes a pig or a couple of sheep.[13]

These descriptions of plenty and of joyous celebration defy accounts of the territory's poverty. Olivia Callwood, eighty-nine, gives a brief description of her 1935 wedding. "My wedding last about two weeks. All was merry and people had a good time. The dress was made in St. Thomas. Albert Soares made my dress. He was a tailor. The cakes were made in St. Thomas, my sisters-in-law and so on made them. The parties were held up by Mrs. Chinnery."

According to Eileene Parsons, "weddings went on for days because the bride's people kept the wedding and then the groom's people kept the wedding." Women played the dominant role in these family/community activities as seamstresses, cooks, and pastry makers. Parsons, a former minister for Health, Education, and Welfare, describes her experiences as a flower girl in the 1930s and 1940s.

For Miss Pheen's wedding I think it was Blanche Titley who made my dress. I know my little hat was made by Miss Loubelle Penn. Alice Jennings was the person who dressed brides and the little flower girls. She lived in the area by where McKelly's is now and you would dress there, then go down to the church. Then when the wedding was over everybody walked. You would walk up to Huntum's Ghut. When I was my aunt Docy's flower girl, we walked up to Fahie Hill and although you were the little flower girl you had to help the bridesmaid hold up this long train because it couldn't drag on the ground. In those days when the banns were announced the parents of the bride and friends would start saving eggs because everybody had fowl. People would give things like flour and family would save your goat and pigs and calf because it was days of feasting. In Pheen's case and my aunt Docy's a great big tent was built and the bride and groom were seated and toasts were made. They were big weddings. In those days the top-level cooks were this lady at Fort Hill, Miss Emma Fahie, my great-aunt Mamselle, Catherine Malone, my grandmother, a lady who was living by the burial ground, Miss Kate. They were the top-notch cooks of the day and the cake-makers. They would go from village to village. They would be there with their big aprons, they cooked in kerosene tins. The cakes were baked in brick ovens. This cooking would happen in the different villages and people would send the stuff to the family.[14]

In these ways women provided important links between communities and at the same time created and strengthened bonds between each other. The goodwill of communities toward other communities rested heavily on the work that women put into organizing social activities such as weddings. Weddings were opportunities for family members and others to reaffirm ties and encourage social homogeneity. They were also occasions for reinforcing family pride and family identity. Since some families predominated in certain communities, such as the Kline and Donovan families of Carrot Bay, family pride translated into community pride. A wedding was thus a chance to do both the family and the community proud.

Women were also prominent at other community gatherings. Hoeing large plots of land, preparing a site for a new house (many were still being built of thatch until the middle part of the twentieth century), and boat launchings were community affairs. Groups of women would work in the kitchen or over the coal pots while the men did the hammering or the digging. Some women often led in singing the work songs by which the men found the rhythm of their work. When, at last, the women gave the signal that the fish and fungi, the mutton and the dove pork, the rum and coconut water were ready, work ceased and the real socializing got under way.

Obeah as a traditional practice also continued to play a role in the lives of the people, and here again, women continued to be involved. A 1904 Obeah Act banning its practice had little effect. Under the act, "any person who pretends or professes to tell fortunes, or uses any subtle craft, means or device, by palmistry or otherwise, or pretends to cure injuries or diseases or to intimidate or effect any purpose by means of any charm, incantation or other pretended supernatural practise, shall be liable to be imprisoned for any period not exceeding six months." On the other hand, any person "practising, or in any way concerned in the practise of obeah, or using any subtle craft, means of device by obeah or otherwise shall be liable to be imprisoned for any period not exceeding *twelve months*." Colonial authorities were trying to make a subtle distinction between "supernatural practices" and "obeah," which they seemed to believe was more dangerous. Even composing, writing, printing, selling, distributing, publishing, or circulating material "calculated to promote the superstition of obeah" was an offense. People found guilty were subject to either six months' imprisonment or a fine of $240, a prohibitive sum for many prior to the 1980s. (The law remains on the books today.) But belief in obeah persisted. Fishlock, writing in 1912, said that "this belief, though not manifested in any conspicuous manner, still affects the life of the people and has considerable influence on their actions. Salutary legislation, together with the infliction of severe punishment on so-called obeah [practitioners] is, however, having a good effect, in helping to stamp out this pernicious belief." Fishlock's confidence, like Porter's in the previous century, was simply wishful thinking.

Decades later Trevor describes an account related to him. "A man called_____ who lived on Chalwell Estate had a spirit put on him and a lady from Sea Cows Bay went to take it off. [Witnesses] saw the woman continually chewing a long black cloth and after a while some part of the spirit fastened in this. . . . The woman pulled the spirit to her and put him in a jim-john [demijohn] and from that night the man was not tormented."

But obeah was losing ground. As Africa receded further and further from the community's collective consciousness, obeah's importance to the people's spiritual life diminished. It was no longer seen as the refuge of first resort. Instead, it was Christianity, particularly Methodism, that dominated people's lives. "On the outskirts of Town was a huge Tamarind. In its umber shade there appeared to be human figures. These were good Wesleyans. From distant coral bays and towering mountain ridges they had tramped, barefoot, carrying their shoes, stockings and Sunday finery upon their heads. One . . . woman was pulling on a pair of flesh pink silk stockings. Another was struggling to insert her . . . foot into a pointed-toed, high-heeled shoe."[15] The scene was repeated in other parts of the territory. Elmore Stoutt recalls that, for members of the Zion Hill Methodist Church in the western end of Tortola, it was a "usual sight to see women, especially from the Northside, changing their flat shoes, after walking miles, to high heels which were only meant for the church yard and in the church."

Women's commitment and dedication to their religion was, in fact, the foundation of their church's strength.

During the period between the destruction of the [Cane Garden Bay] Chapel and its rebuilding [1924–1925] worship services were held in the home of Mrs. Ann Elizabeth Rhymer, who though not a local preacher acted as such when inclement weather prevented accredited Local Preachers keeping their appointments to conduct services on Sundays. Mrs. Rhymer who was assisted by Mrs. Josephine Hodge is regarded as the member who did much to keep the flame of Methodism burning in Cane Garden Bay.[16]

In communities throughout the Virgin Islands, women placed their labor, their time, and their property at the disposal of their churches. In Carrot Bay the homes of women such as Martha Callwood, Rebecca Skelton, Amanda Donavan, and Henrietta Dawson were the meeting houses for Sunday evening worship. Quite likely these women and others like them were hosts of many of the all-night prayer meetings that missionaries had attempted to discourage in the 1800s but that continued to flourish at least until the 1950s.[17]

Given their industry and dedication, it is ironic that these women, like all their sisters, were excluded from the possibility of becoming reverends or pastors. Churches benefited from women's labor but denied them equal opportunities with men to form the top leadership of the church.

In fact, patriarchy colluded with colonialist paternalism to result in the denigration of women and their achievements throughout Virgin Islands society. A quick look at references to women in the colony's only newspaper in the 1960s, The Tortola Times, and in the newsletter of the Social Welfare Council, The Torch, is revealing. Commenting on the achievement of a schoolteacher who won an award, the editor of The Tortola Times wrote that "some women have both brains and beauty." Women's looks were of great interest to the one-man operation that was The Tortola Times; several times, in mentioning the appointments of women as teachers, nurses, and so forth, they were described as "beautiful" or "attractive." Similarly, in discussing women, the editor appeared always careful to emphasize those attributes and interests that conformed to patriarchal notions of the attributes and interests best befitting women. The hobbies of Festival Queen candidates were often listed as "needlework" and "cooking," indicating not only women's submission to societal expectations of them but, by highlighting them, acting also as a subtle reward. Articles on the appointments of men mentioned neither their physical attributes nor their hobbies but focused, instead, on their qualifications and experience.

The Tortola Times was not alone in this. An article in The Torch is written in a similar vein:

Miss Flavie O'Neal is our Virgin Gorda correspondent. She, too, is a young school-teacher on the staff of St. Mary's School. Her interests, however, extend beyond the walls of the classroom, and she finds time to play the organ and practice cooking.
"Cooking," she says, "fascinates me."
Her ambition is to study medicine and become a doctor.[18]

This schoolteacher's interests as both a correspondent for the paper and in medicine receive short shrift, whereas her more traditional interests are highlighted. She is allowed to speak for herself when she speaks of cooking but not when she talks about her career hopes.[19] Still, it is possible here to see women's resistance; cooking might well have fascinated her, but it is obvious that her professional ambitions were what drove her to seek academic success.

Women were not unaware of their secondary status in the society. Even as Virgin Islands men raged against the limitations posed by the colonial system to their political leadership, women chafed against restrictions that limited their public or political participation on terms of equality with men. An editorial in *The Tortola Times* declared that:

After the recent sitting of the Supreme Court at Road Town a number of citizens have brought up an old question for discussion—is it not time for the women of the BVI to play their part by being allowed to serve jury duty?

A number of ladies have voiced this opinion quite strongly to the Editor and have given a variety of sound reasons in support of their argument . . .

In this colony only men resident in Tortola between the ages of 21 and 60 are eligible for jury service. There is also an income or property owning qualification that is so small that it includes practically every working male on the island.

That the jury are the undisputed judges of fact by democratic tradition is only too well-known and the cry for equality in every sphere of life raises the question in feminine minds "Do we not have the same mental attributes as men to decide on facts put before us? Do we not reason just as soundly and fairly?"

Jury service is a civic duty and an honourable function for the safeguard of human rights and liberties. We must reflect on the possibilities of the fairer sex making their contribution to law, order and above all justice.[20]

The only concession the editor makes to women's ambition is to "reflect" on the possibility of granting them a privilege that men had held for years. The editor's use of the term "fairer sex" suggests that his idea of women as fragile and gentle precluded him from coming to the immediate conclusion that women could contribute to the stern demands of law, order, and justice.

Womanliness was identified most strongly with motherhood. A 2 July 1960 article in *The Tortola Times* advocating family planning noted that "many women in the BVI are leading lives that are spoiled by physical and mental strain because they had too many babies; some women have had over twenty children."

The importance of children to Virgin Islands society in those years can be understood by looking at the terms used to define children's provenance or what one author called the "degrees of parenthood." Virgin Islanders had subtle ways of distinguishing between children. "'Own' children are those by man and wife; 'yard' children are those by a woman (married or not) and a man other than her husband but who has been a friend for a long time; 'bush' children are those by a woman and a casual acquaintance; 'spree' children—father unknown," explains a woman from the country." [21]

This nonjudgmental and precise delineation or categorization highlights the point that motherhood was of even higher importance than marriage. "The infertile woman, or the woman with few children, is even today on the whole despised by her fellows," wrote one observer.[22] Put in a situation where there were few alternatives open to her, maternity was the sole outcome for the majority of Virgin Islands women. But illegitimacy was not viewed benignly by the colonial authorities. The following is an extract from a brief address given by Administrator Martin S. Stavely in 1962.

It is impossible to overstress the importance of a happy marriage relationship. Children of a happy marriage may not always turn out well, but they will have a better chance of doing so than children of parents who are divided or separated or unfaithful to one another.

But unfortunately our problems go even deeper than those resulting from a broken or unhappy marriage. Many of our children also have never known married parents, some have never known their fathers. I cannot too strongly condemn these casual liaisons, which are such a scrounge [sic] in these islands. They are harmful to the persons concerned, they are harmful to the children and they are harmful to the society itself. It is perhaps the greatest evil we have to contend with. I would especially like to condemn the idea that is prevalent that a woman is not a woman until she has a child, usually before marriage is even considered. This is not only the most utter nonsense, it has done tremendous harm to our community and has caused endless unhappiness especially for the unfortunate children who result from such adventures. It is nonsense because so many of the finest women who ever lived have been unmarried and childless such as Florence Nightingale and Elizabeth Fry.[23]

But the importance Europeans attached to conventional or middle-class forms of marriage was not felt by islanders. For centuries, during slavery, marriage among slaves was discouraged and unrecognized by colonial authorities; African marriage forms were not appreciated and Christian marriages among slaves were not acknowledged. Slave families were sometimes disrupted by sales or removal. This history militated against a full adoption or embrace of European-style marriage, which continued well past emancipation and, arguably, exists today. In addition, as was previously noted, many black women feared the changes formal marriage would bring to their relationships.

Proudfoot claims that "the dislike of West Indian women for a formal marriage bond is deeply rooted in tradition." In fact, the option to marry did not reside with the majority of women, and some women certainly did desire formal marriage. But Proudfoot is not entirely wrong. As we have already seen in previous chapters, there were women who strongly resisted marriage and the subjugation it would entail. Travel writer Eleanor Early recalls the "reigning belle of Road Town" telling her she "had better sense than to tie she-self to a man. . . . A woman's a fool to sell she-self out. Once a man git her marry wif him, he git her good. Then he forget her for true. If she ain married wif him, he remember she." It is also possible that some of the women who were reluctant to consider marriage may have been successful entrepreneurs of their communities who did not wish to lose their autonomy. In any case, women were well aware that it was motherhood that conferred womanly status, not marriage.

Economic factors may also have led to at least a deferral of marriage. Proudfoot notes that "marriage in the eyes of the average West Indian peasant is a ceremony which should only be indulged in by those who are economically secure." According to her, married men could not expect their wives to do field work. Once married it was expected that the woman would confine her activities to the home. In that way, her confinement and removal from the field indicated the man's status and the couple's passage into middle-class respectability. A late formal marriage, with its perceived conferral of status and dignity, could be seen as the woman's reward for long-standing productive and reproductive service. But this observation of Proudfoot's may have applied only to middle-class blacks or blacks with middle-class aspirations—in the Virgin Islands many women continued to work throughout their lives.

Constrained by maternity and/or marriage, women were more than twice removed from transcending their existence in a society ruled from afar. Barely able to lay claim to a sense of self as Subject, Virgin Islands women found it difficult to lay claim to their country. In an agricultural community land represents the transformative potential, the possibility of home ownership, of agricultural, commercial, and thereby other forms of development. Though women worked the land, they often could not participate in this identification as men could and did. Women's access to land and thus their ability to participate in a Virgin Islands identity founded on land ownership was frequently dependent on men. Women had owned land even in slavery, but property ownership legislation did not give them equal rights with men, particularly when it came to inheritance.

Maurer recounts a story from the 1920s that illustrates the havoc this aspect of patriarchy could wreak on women's lives.

Rebecca had [been living on family land] with her husband and two sons. She had also been looking after the upbringing of the four siblings who remained with her . . . described as "children." The remaining three siblings were abroad . . . two of her sisters had been living and working in Santo Domingo and the third . . . in St. Thomas. These three sisters together earned the only steady income in the family, sending remittances back in order to pay the land tax and, at their mother's death, her funeral costs. Rebecca and her husband eked out a living making charcoal and baking bread, which it seems they traded locally.[24]

Then Rebecca's brother returned with his family, claimed all the land for himself, and evicted his siblings. He could do so because inheritance laws before 1945 provided for the estate of a parent who died without a will to pass entirely to the heir-at-law or firstborn son.

Similarly, women in common-law unions could claim no legal right to property that was in the man's name, even if she had contributed to its development. When the man in a common-law union died intestate, the woman could not get a share in the property. (The situation remains unchanged.)

Surprisingly, women's precarious claim to land did not stop one woman's prominent involvement in the most important campaign involving land issues in the territory in this century. In 1964, what became known as the Bates-Hill Agreement was signed between the government and the Bates-Hill Company, a British development corporation. The agreement, essentially a 199-year lease, gave Bates-Hill control of Wickham's Cay, which was to become a sizeable chunk of real estate in Road Town. The agreement also gave the company a lease for three-quarters of Anegada. Although the deal was initially greeted with favor, public opposition began to build after people heard that "the only black people that would be allowed to go on Wickham's Cay were the maids."

Several of the community's younger residents took exception to this plan and began to rally opposition to the agreement. Patsy Lake, a salon owner, joined forces with Noel Lloyd, Lindy De Castro (Ras Uhuru), Wilfred Smith, and a few others, including Luella Harrigan, Roosevelt Smith, and Cromwell Nibbs. They held regular meetings at Lake's house to discuss the agreement and new developments. The group began to call itself the Positive Action Movement (PAM). Public meetings were held in the evenings at the Old Recreation Ground. PAM leaders called for mass protests. In days, demonstrators marched on the chief minister's office and on Government House. The marches often ended in confrontations with the police, during which some of the leaders were arrested and rearrested. But more and more people joined the protests. In all, at least ten marches were organized to demand the abrogation of the agreement. Britain grew so concerned it sent a battleship.

"We saw the deal as a sellout of the rights of the people, not as encouragement to investors," says Lake. "We could see, given the terms of the agreement, why Bates felt he could keep us off the land. Wickham's Cay was supposed to be an island and blacks weren't welcome unless they came to clean."

The agreement was dissolved in 1970, two years after the demonstrations began.

Lake's participation in a fight to reclaim land for Virgin Islanders at a time when women's own rights to land were only gradually being acknowledged was exceptional. In fighting to establish Virgin Islanders' patrimonial rights to the Wickham's Cay area, Lake unknowingly staked a claim for all women's right to associate their identity with the land on equal terms with men. Certainly she was the first woman to assume a prominent position in a popular movement in this century. That this movement was also the first to deal with land issues reveals the fact that women, whatever the customs and whatever the legislation, also felt that they too had some claim to the land.

A report from 1970 stressed the importance of land to Virgin Islanders.

A large proportion of British Virgin Islanders are landowners and a family that does not own two acres of land is rare. To them the land has become more than the basic means of production; it is a symbol of their independence and the key to that independence. No real understanding of recent events in this territory is possible unless the role that land plays in the psychology of the Virgin Islands is firmly grasped.[25]

The Bates-Hill Agreement challenged this identification and sparked a national movement. Lake's participation symbolized women's broader participation in this identification. At the same time, Lake's activism placed her among the more than a few women who managed to impose their presence and leadership in several key fields that contributed to the shaping of Virgin Islands society.

Women's ability to assume leadership roles, in the face of significant obstacles posed by patriarchy, the paternalism of colonialism, and colonialism itself, is ample testimony to their courage and dedication to the territory and its future.

NOTES

1. The Executive Council consisted of the governor, the colonial secretary, the attorney general, the commissioner, and several official and unofficial members. The first three were headquartered in Antigua, whereas the others resided on Tortola. In the governor's absence, the commissioner presided over the council. Norwell Harrigan and Pearl Varlack, *The Virgin Islands Story* (Essex: Caribbean Universities Press in association with Bowker Publishing, 1975), p. 151.

2. Joan French, *Women and Colonial Policy after the 1938 Uprising in Jamaica* (Kingston: University of the West Indies, 1989), p. 124. The West India Royal Commission was appointed by the British government in 1938 to investigate conditions in the English-speaking Caribbean following a series of disturbances and demonstrations in most of the islands, including the BVI. It was headed by Lord Moyne and also was known as the Moyne Commission.

3. Political Report of the Leeward Islands, March 1955. *CO 1031/1811.* According to this report, in 1955, the minimum wage in the USVI stood at $4.50, whereas in the Virgin Islands it was $1.50. (That year it was raised to $1.75.) The College of the Virgin Islands report, published in the 1960s, states, however, that in the fifties domestic workers were making 18 to 20 cents an hour, hotel and restaurant workers were collecting 30 to 35 cents an hour, and construction workers were being paid from 80 cents to $1.00. Hugh Smith, assistant director of VI Employment Security Agency in *The Alien Worker and His Family,* Proceedings of a Conference (St. Thomas: College of the Virgin Islands, 1967), p. 7. The disparity in these reports may have been caused by a misunderstanding of the dollar's valuation as opposed to the pound.

4. A report also listed "lucrative employment on the sugar estates in Santo Domingo" and the "large profits on the sale of wine and liquor to purchasers from Puerto Rico and [the USVI]" as contributing to the economy of the Virgin Islands. (This was during Prohibition in America.) Captain F. W. Griffith, "The Agricultural Conditions Prevailing in the British Virgin Islands," 1932. *CO 152/423/16.*

5. The Leeward Islands governor reported in 1936 that, on a visit to the territory, he "was met by constant lamentations by the people . . . that they were becoming more and more imprisoned . . . by the prohibitions on the US mainland or the American islands or Santo Domingo to engage in work or by tariff difficulties in selling produce in foreign lands." Report by Governor John Lethem, 23 July 1936. *CO 152/465/16.*

6. A leading politician of that time who later sat on the Legislative Council remembered women as not having been given the vote in that constitution. Howard Penn, *Memoirs of H. R. Penn: A Personal Account of the History and Politics of the BVI in the 20th Century* (Road Town: N.p., n.d), p. 30. According to Penn, suffrage for women came in 1953. This may have been wishful thinking since Mr. Penn was chairman of the constitutional meeting at which it was recommended that only men who met certain property and literacy qualifications be granted the vote.

7. This was the first political party formed in the Virgin Islands and, like its successors, was nothing more than a vehicle for election, an alliance of prominent men determined to hold political office. Thus do parties in the territory have what Duverger terms a "parliamentary origin"; for them election to office is the "essence of the life of the party, the very reason for its existence and the supreme purpose of its life." He identifies parties of this sort with the early phases of democracy. Maurice Duverger, *Political Parties: Their Organisation and Activity in the Modern State* (Paris, 1950; rpt., London: Methuen and Co., 1931), p. xxxv.

8. In the meantime, colonial authorities were congratulating themselves on their successful experiment. The governor of the Leeward Islands boasted that the past year "has seen the introduction of means whereby the elected members in all the four Presidencies can exercise a far greater influence on Government policies and can keep a far closer watch on the execution of those policies . . . The impact made by the elected members as Chairman of Committees in Antigua, Montserrat and the Virgin Islands has been considerable." "Extract from the Address by the Governor to the General Legislative Council of the Leeward Islands," 6 January 1953, in Ann Spackman, *Constitutional Developments of the West Indies 1922–1968: A Selection from the Major Documents* (Essex: Caribbean Universities Press in association with Bowker Publishing, 1975), pp. 208–209.

9. Spackman, p. 209. Though elected members were allocated subject areas on which they could propose policy, the heads of government departments remained British expatriate men or men from other Caribbean islands.

10. "Extract from Address by the Governor to the General Legislative Council of the Leeward Islands," 6 January 1953 in Spackman, *Constitutional Development*, pp. 208–209.

11. *West India Royal Commission Report (Moyne Report)* (London: HMSO, 1945), p. 461. These included the Teacher's Association, represented by Norwell Harrigan, O. Flax, and C. S. Elmes, and the Virgin Islands Civic League, represented by H. A. Abbott, Joseph R. O'Neal, and Howard R. Penn.

12. Interview with Ilva Lettsome, 6 August 1998. Interview by author, Paraquita Bay.

13. William Maurer, *Recharting the Caribbean: Land, Law and Citizenship in the British Virgin Islands* (Michigan: UMM Dissertation Services, 1994), p. 20.

14. Interview with Eileene Parsons, 12 August 1998. Interview by author, Road Town.

15. Hazel Ballance Eadie, *Lagooned in the Virgin Islands* (London: George Routledge and Sons, 1931), p. 76.

16. Woodie Blackman, *Methodism: 200 Years in the British Virgin Islands* (Bridgetown: BVI Methodist Church, 1989), p. 102.

17. For more on this, see J. C. Trevor, *Aspects of Folk Culture in the Virgin Islands*, Ph.D. diss., 1950, pp. 48–49. According to him, "as many as a hundred people may attend" these meetings, which "last as a rule from eight o'clock at night until six o'clock the following morning."

18. *The Torch* 2, no. 6 (September 1949). The Social Welfare Council, which published *The Torch*, was a vigorous proponent of greater internal self-government. When it became clear at the end of 1949 that the colonial authority was prepared to grant this wish, the council began to express concern that leadership would be in the hands of women, as noted in the section on women in education.

19. That women did not escape internalizing the roles expected of them is, of course, also evident in the quote. It is quite likely that Flavie O'Neal understood the challenge to patriarchal authority posed by her ambition and sought to placate public opinion by mentioning her more traditional interest.

20. *Tortola Times*, 11 April 1959, p. 3.

21. Robb White, *Our Virgin Island* (London: Victor Gollancz Ltd., 1953), p. 46.

22. Mary Proudfoot, *Britain and the United States in the Caribbean* (London: Faber and Faber, 1954), p. 88.

23. "Mothers' Union Christian Family Service: Address by His Honour, the Administrator," *Island Sun*, 29 December 1962.

24. Maurer, p. 64.

25. *Report of the British Virgin Islands* (London: HMSO, 1970), p. 6.

CHAPTER 6

Public Lives

WOMEN AND WELFARE

Governor Sir Gilbert Rennie warned the Lusaka Business and Professional Women's Club in a speech that "the family is the basis of our social structure and any undermining of that basis will imperil the future welfare and prosperity of the country." He encouraged white colonial women to pay attention to social service and voluntary work that would give "the home . . . its proper place in our lives."[1] In fact, he expected white women's activism in the colonies to be aimed at imparting middle-class European women's domestic ideals to native women. White colonial women were thus seen as the heirs apparent to the legacy of nineteenth-century abolitionists who sought to remake the slave family in the image of the middle-class English family. These efforts were particularly concentrated on native women, seen perhaps as the most amenable to instruction. (Also, European women had often been stereotyped as the civilizing sex, the gentler sex, capable of calming men's savage passions. Getting to native women may have been seen as a way of getting to the men.) Since black women had been excluded for so long from participating in the rarefied ideology of European womanhood, it could also be argued by colonials that they had the most catching up to do.

European women in the Virgin Islands may have been unaware of Sir Gilbert's speech, but they did not shirk their duty. Alberta Brodie, a Belgian woman, who purchased and lived on Beef Island in the 1890s, taught many East End young women Paraquin lace making. This skill was passed from woman to woman until many in the territory became proficient in it.

Brodie was not the only colonial woman to encourage lace making. Jenkins, visiting the islands in 1913, reported that, "Mrs. Jarvis, the Commissioner's wife, had started lace-making among the women and had aroused some interest in the work."

Lace making, a delicate craft, and lace in general are closely associated with European femininity. It was one of several hobbies with which women were expected to occupy themselves in the home during their spare time. But Virgin Islands women used this craft as a source of income. Early mentions "the exquisite lacework that the women of Tortola do" that could be seen at the cooperative in Charlotte Amalie, St. Thomas. By using lace making as a moneymaking enterprise, Virgin Islands women demonstrated their involvement in the public sphere of commerce on however limited a basis. Unaccustomed to a rigid and impermeable division of private and public spheres, families in the Virgin Islands depended equally on men and women's labor for their sustenance and survival. Any new skill women learned was almost certainly going to be put toward earning more income.

British women who visited the territory for a relatively short time also felt obligated to pick up the white woman's burden. Englishwoman Hazel Balance Eadie and her friend Ann Churchill visited the Virgin Islands sometime in the 1920s. During their stay Eadie founded a Boys' Club, a Girls' Club, and the Excelsior Cricket Club for Tortola's young men.

Rather romantically, Eadie dreamed that the boys and girls in her clubs would grow up "with natures sunny and lively as the sparkling waves that broke on their coral bays . . . [with wills] as strong and unmovable as their high mountains and [with] minds pure and stainless as the fragrant white blossoms that starred the bush." The club's motto was "to grow upwards," toward God, as she explained it. Thirty was the age limit for membership. In all, about four clubs were formed, one each in Road Town, Sea Cows Bay, Kingstown, and Cane Garden Bay. Eadie hoped they would help counteract what she called the "appalling" educational system at the time. The education grant from the British then amounted to £447, less than half of the amount allocated to agriculture, £939.

Despite her romanticism, Eadie's enthusiasm was genuine. After paying visits to the different schools on Tortola, none of which impressed her, Eadie decided a complaint to the authorities was in order:

I launched an epistle [to the Commissioner] . . . describing the educational state of the island and pleading that the hopelessly inadequate educational funds might be increased. I pictured the lives of the children and adolescents in those parts of the Island, where there were no schools, nor anything to counteract the influence of the many undesirable factors in heredity and environment. In the role of prophetess, I foretold that their unenlightened state would prove a menace to the future of the islands, since the children had no chance of growing up into worthy citizens of Empire, and I ended thus "It seems to me that any expenditure that prevents human wastage and wreckage must prove in the end to be true economy."

The commissioner to whom she had written (probably R. Hargrove, who came and went in 1923) left soon after she sent the letter she describes, but she took up the matter with his successor (probably Captain O. L. Hancock). She did not get a sympathetic hearing. "He said that education merely made them discontented with their lot and disrespectful to the white man. Let the misguided people who tried to educate them out of their proper plane go elsewhere."

Despite this discouragement Eadie persevered with her youth clubs. Her efforts culminated in a big youth rally on the Recreation Ground before the commissioner and other dignitaries. She and Churchill left the island soon after.

A couple of decades later, Edith Wailing the wife of Commissioner Dr. Donald Percy Wailing started the Home Industries Committee to help raise funds for World War II while helping women sell products ranging from straw hats to jams and jellies. The committee was similar to the women's institutes operating on some of the other islands.[2] According to French, these institutes originated in Canada and were introduced into Britain during World War I. Farmers' wives and daughters were organized to support the war effort by producing vegetables, small livestock, and so on, which they sold to each other. Meetings consisted of talks on health and child care, and sessions on cooking, how to make preserves, sewing, and knitting. Trinidadian feminist Rhoda Reddock believes self-help movements such as these "encouraged and facilitated economic activities centred around the 'womanly skills' which all women were supposed to have learnt in their homes." Organizations similar to the committee in aims and objectives were also established in Jamaica and some of the other islands.

In the Virgin Islands the government provided the women participating in the program, most of whom came from East End, with a small building, free of charge, from which the goods were sold. This was in the Market Square, now known as the Sir Olva Georges Plaza.

Linda O'Neal, a Road Town resident at the time, recollects that "Mrs. Wailing wanted to help the war effort and also to help the people here with their crafts and skills. She got the ladies from East End who were more into hat making and needlework, mainly lace making which was started with Mrs. Brodie, and she had them bring in their work, their hats and bags made of straw."

The goods were sold primarily to local people, though the then infrequent tourists were also customers.

Mabel Titley, daughter of Emmeline Titley, who ran the shop, says that "apart from making the hats and bags they also did yards of plaits which were shipped to St. Thomas for sale."[3] Again, Virgin Islands women were turning their craft skills into valuable income-generating industries. Though no figures are available to establish the value of these craft exports, their impact on participants' income would not have been negligible.

The Home Industries Shop continued to exist long after World War II ended. A 1955/1956 government report noted that "a fair quantity of straw and basket work is produced for sale through a local agency in Road Town called the 'Home Industries Shop' which is operated for the benefit of the producers. This work is also exported to St. Thomas. This industry does not receive any Government assistance."

Mrs. Wailing was also one of the women who started the Girl Guides movement in the Virgin Islands. Guiding was very much a British import without much deference to its local context. Patrols were named after things common in the English countryside but unknown in the Virgin Islands, such as Snowdrops, Forget-me-nots, and Robins.

Although the Guiding organization fostered an element of adventure with its camps and hikes, it also served to reinforce conventional ideas about women's roles. Ethel Smith remembers that "in order to get a badge the Guides had to get the dirtiest piece of laundry they could find and wash it as clean as they could." The Guides combined an inculcation in "womanly duties" with another tradition long associated with women's restricted public role—welfare work. To get their sewing badge, Girl Guides had to sew an outfit for a child from a disadvantaged family. Unlike Eadie's clubs, the Guides with their tea parties would appear, at least initially, to have been mostly a club for girls from the territory's middle classes, many of whom came from Road Town.

Like Mrs. Wailing, the other wives of twentieth-century commissioners or governors identified their role within a specific traditional and/or maternal sphere. They often served as presidents of the BVI Red Cross with its strictly welfare orientation. There they helped to create programs for disabled people and for the elderly and/or sick. The Red Cross Baby Show, which could be won by participants on the basis of health, weight, and appearance, was an annual event organized by the club. Although programs such as these may have had the laudable intention of encouraging good nutrition and parenting skills, they also served to underscore a preoccupation with conventional expectations of women. At the same time, the unwritten expectation that the wives of governors must, perforce, assume the presidency of the organization reinforced and demonstrated traditional patriarchal expectations of women's public roles.

The BVI Red Cross was started in 1956 by Virgin Islanders, the majority of whom were women. The first president was Marie O'Neal, and the early membership included local women such as Margaret Borde, Adina Donovan, and Thelma Swain. (A few men were also active in the organization.) Initial activities included helping the needy in the community, organizing blood-donor drives, conducting first aid courses, and visiting hospital and infirmary patients on Tortola and Virgin Gorda. Coopting the wife of the queen's representative lent status and prestige to these maternal activities.

Wives of colonial administrators have also busied themselves with handicraft projects or dedicated themselves to gardening, albeit on a national scale. Commissioner Martin S. Staveley's wife was said to be "keenly interested in the development of local handicrafts," whereas Mary Barwick, wife of Governor David Barwick, played a major role in creating the Botanic Gardens in Road Town. In these ways, colonial wives made themselves of service to the community in nonthreatening ways. Originating in cosmopolitan countries where women had long demanded equal rights with men, the wives of colonial administrators nevertheless made (and make) themselves as unobtrusive as possible in the Virgin Islands. In identifying their roles so narrowly, they have consciously or unconsciously helped to reinforce patriarchal myths about woman's role within the family and within the society. They fulfill the middle-class patriarchal ideal of the stay-at-home wife whose activities outside the home do not threaten gender conventions. Jobless, they are still the incorporated wives of a bygone era, totally dependent on their husbands and without an identity of their own within modern colonial society.

The very fact that governors, and before them, commissioners, have all been men points to patriarchal colonial policies that hearken back to the early practices of the Foreign Office. Female clerical and executive officers were not employed there on a permanent basis until 1921 and had to leave the service upon marriage. Although the United Kingdom's Sex Disqualification (Removal) Act of 1919 stated that nobody should be disqualified "by sex or marriage from the exercise of any public function," it also contained provisions allowing certain branches or posts to be reserved for men. Subsequent regulations made in 1921 specifically restricted to men all posts in the United Kingdom's Diplomatic and Consular Services. Arguments suggesting that women were well-suited to the colonial service because of an affinity for social and philanthropic duties were met by counterarguments that these duties were already being performed by the wives and daughters of colonial officials without any cost to the state. The state, through the wives of colonial officials, was essentially getting the work of "two diplomatists . . . for more or less the price of one." It was not until 1946 that women were finally allowed to enter the administrative grade of the Foreign Service on a permanent basis. They were, however, limited to 10 percent of the total intake in any one year and were paid 20 percent less than men for the same work. (Equal pay for women was not introduced until almost a decade later, in 1955. The marriage bar was rescinded in 1972, but until 1985, all the women in the most senior diplomatic posts were unmarried.) Despite these advances in the mother country, colonial wives in the Virgin Islands hew closely to the tradition of supplementing the work of their husbands.

Their lack of paid employment and their lives of comparative ease are in stark contrast to that of Virgin Islands women. During the 1930 and 1940s, the migration of men was reaching its peak, with the majority finding work on the military bases under construction in the U.S. Virgin Islands. Women also were migrating. Some found work on the bases, but the majority of female migrants went into domestic service, as will be discussed later. The number of women leaving the territory in these years did not approach that of men.

In 1938, the Moyne Commission wrote that "busy as they are with problems of labour, health and education [colonial governments] have naturally been content to leave the work of social welfare to any who were willing to undertake it." The colonial authorities were not actually very busy with education (or much else) in the Virgin Islands. Rather, Britain's neglect of the territory created a leadership vacuum that women filled in education, health, and welfare.

In the early 1950s, Eugenie Todman-Smith, a teacher at Belle Vue, started a parent-teacher association there and subsequently at the other schools where she taught. She recollects that

The United Nations used to send these kegs of dried milk to the territory but the government had no money to transport them to the schools so they would only go to the schools if the schools could get them there. So through the Belle Vue association we got the parents to arrange to bring the milk from Road Town. They did this with two mules who carried the kegs on poles tied up between them. Another project the association got involved in was providing water to the school. There was no water at the school so children had to go and bring water from a ghut someplace. That was hard. Those who brought it were usually those who lived near the school. The association got permission from the government to get water from the nearby cistern which was probably used for the cattle dip. That was an ease.[4]

Todman-Smith later became the territory's community development officer responsible for furthering social development and replacing outmoded ways of thinking and doing. One of her tasks was to persuade people in Cane Garden Bay to stop using the beach there as a toilet.

Several individual women on their own initiative and without governmental assistance began programs in their communities that continue today. In 1950, Valerie Thomas formed the St. Paul's Junior Club to give the young members of her community "a sense of purpose." Up until then she had been a Sunday school teacher, the organist at St. Paul's Anglican Church in Sea Cows Bay (on the outskirts of Road Town), the choir mistress, and a member of the church-sponsored Mother's Union. Children who joined the club were taught public speaking, cake making, and handwork. In 1957, disturbed by the lack of reading material in the community, she organized club members into a construction team, and a small library was built on her property. Priests who had once served in the territory and visitors to the island were solicited for book donations. By the end of the year, more than 300 books had been received. Until the Department of Library Services instituted its bookmobile service in the 1960s, the Sea Cows Bay Community Library created by Thomas was the main source of books for both children and adults in the area.

Thomas was also active in the women's organization of her church, the Mother's Union. The union focused on women's role within the family and home by holding talks and organizing activities around the subjects of motherhood and homemaking. A Christian Family Week organized by the union in 1962, for instance, aimed to discuss the issues of "discipline in the family; courtesy and the family; and the Christian's private and public responsibility."

In 1963, when the Mother's Union changed its name to Women of the Church and allowed single and/or childless women to be members, Thomas became president.

The union, like other voluntary associations in which women participated and assumed leadership roles, was a means of entering the public sphere. Through their voluntary work, women contributed to the development of the territory and staked their claim to citizenship. The recognition of colonial authorities often followed. In 1973, Thomas was awarded the British Empire Medal for her work in establishing the Junior Club and the Community Library. She was the ninth woman to receive that honor. The Junior Club is still in existence today.

Volunteerism was strongly ingrained in women's character. One man recounts his wife's contribution to their community. "In 1960 . . . my wife volunteered to serve as a sub-post mistress free of charge. She performed this service for over ten years . . . the government eventually recognized her officially as Sub-Post Mistress with a peanut salary."[5]

In fact, it was almost exclusively through their volunteer work that women, particularly married women, could have an impact on public policy and on their society. Only in 1947 did the colonial secretary abolish the regulation that married women were ineligible by reason of their marriage for appointments to established posts in the civil service.[6] Up until that time women who already held such posts were required to resign upon marriage. Shut out of the easiest and most obvious avenue to public life, married women devised other means through which to influence their society.[7]

On 25 January 1968, several women attended the first meeting of what became known as the BVI Community league. There are two important points to be made about the League. One, it was formed exclusively of women from the social elite of the territory. Six of the seven women present were the wives and/or sisters of Road Town's prominent men, political leaders, businessmen, and doctors.[8] In 1965, one of the members, Emmogene Creque, had become the first woman to sit on the Legislative Council. She was nominated to the position when nominated member Joseph R. O'Neal had to be away on leave. At the time, her husband, Henry Creque, was also a member of the council. The lone single woman, and the only one not from town, was the territory's librarian, Verna Penn. The second important point about the league was its stated purpose. The league was "devoted to the promotion of the territory's welfare with an emphasis on tourism." The league was not then to be the ordinary volunteer association of women organized around essentially maternal roles.

To the extent that colonial policy saw a public role for women, it envisioned a mere extension of the domestic role. The patriarchal assumption that the financial support of the family necessarily rested on men whereas women were to concern themselves with the care of the children and the home is certainly clear in the Moyne Commission's report. In discussing poverty, the commission wrote that "the consequences of this depression in rural areas are obvious. It is next to impossible for the men to earn enough to support a family with the result that the women have also to work and cannot devote themselves to the maintenance of the home and the care of their children."

The members of the Community League apparently had other ideas. Able to stay at home, isolated and sheltered if they desired to be, these women instead chose active roles in their community—roles, moreover, that were not extensions of their private roles as wives and mothers. According to notes written at its first meeting, the league felt that "priority should be given to the beautification of the surrounding districts and the enlistment of taximen to aid in keeping the territory clean." The librarian was asked to identify places of cultural and/or historical interest that the league would then endeavor to enhance as sites of tourist interest.

Over time the interests of the league broadened. The minutes of a 26 February 1969 meeting record the group's intentions to meet with the chief minister to discuss drainage in Road Town, garbage collection, and the abattoir. The league also wanted to inquire into the government's immigration regulations regarding the screening of new immigrants' health and police records, the maintenance of the post office, the poor water supply at the infirmary, and the cleaning of the Planters Cemetery. These minutes also reveal that the league intended to meet with the welfare officer to discuss the establishment of a home for the aged and the matter of juvenile delinquents.

Clearly, the league interested itself as much in social welfare causes and issues as in wider developmental concerns. In December 1969, the league launched a public appeal for funds to enlarge the infirmary. The league also responded to calls for individual financial assistance to the indigent. In 1968, the league became involved in cultural affairs and organized the Children's Festival.

Their attempts to influence public policy on matters not directly or at all related to women's supposed sphere of domestic or family-related interests were what made the league extraordinary. In 1968, the league called on the government to

make a statement on the proposed organisation, curriculum, and staffing of the new Comprehensive School and in particular as regards a) whether the present teaching staff of the Virgin Islands Secondary School will be absorbed entirely in the Comprehensive School. b) Whether a choice has been made as to the Headteachership (*sic*) of the new school. c) Whether recruitment for additional teaching staff will be advertised in the West Indies and, if so, whether preference will be given to applicants of West Indian origin who possess suitable qualifications. d) Whether any special effort is being made to employ or train suitable *natives* in the school. [emphasis theirs.] e) Whether a system of examinations will be necessary for admission to the Comprehensive School.[9]

The wording of the memorandum at sections c and d suggests a hostility on the part of the league to the appointment of British expatriates. At the time, the major government departments, Public Works, Immigration, Police, and so on were either headed by whites sent from Britain or by people from other Caribbean islands.

That the league's concern that the school and its staff be of good standard is clear. As town residents, many of the league's members had attended the Road Town Methodist School, the best in the colony for many years. League members would have been very aware of the benefits of education. At least one, Leona Harney, had been a schoolteacher trained at the Spring Gardens Teacher's Training College in Antigua.[10]

The league was also worried about immigration issues as their subsequent correspondence with government makes explicit. In a letter sent to the chief minister on 20 March 1968, the league asked for clarification on the government's immigration regulations. Specifically, the group wanted to know if immigrants were required to furnish the following: health and police records, a declaration of purpose for entry and work permits, a statement on duration of visit, and the payment of a required deposit. Finally, wrote the league, it wanted to know "bearing in mind Britain's legislation against immigrants, including West Indians, the number of immigrants who should form our quota, similarly."

At the time of the league's formation the territory was undergoing rapid social, economic, and political change. Significant improvements had been made to the territory's infrastructure, and new hotel developments signaled a turnaround in the territory's economic future. Between 1957 and 1962, the Gross Domestic Product doubled, rising to more than $2 million, and wages were rising. In 1959, the U.S. dollar became the official currency. Attracted by these signs of imminent prosperity, the first immigrants from the other Caribbean islands began trickling in.[11] Many, if not most of them, were either laborers looking for work on various construction sites or domestics looking for jobs primarily in the hotels. They did not belong to the middle and upper classes of their islands and were regarded with suspicion and distrust by league members.

The league also involved itself in efforts to effect the abrogation of the Bates-Hill Agreement discussed earlier. On 18 September 1969 under the presidency of Marie O'Neal, the league submitted a three-page memorandum to the Commission of Inquiry created by the British to investigate the terms of the agreement and survey public opinion on the issue.

The league offered alternatives to the agreement that would also allow for the territory's development. Whereas Article One detailed the league's concerns about flooding in the area, Article Two suggested that the "portion of land situated due West of the Courthouse [which] was advertised as a shopping centre but was given to [Bates-Hill] should be returned to Government" and "used as formerly designated." Article Three proposed that "a part of Wickham's Cay should be retained by Government for the benefit of local residents and disposed of to them at a reasonable cost." Article Four of the league's memorandum suggested, "No part of Wickham's Cay should at any time be kept exclusively for foreign investors." Article Five recommended, "All foreign business coming to Wickham's Cay should be confined to *PIONEER* [emphasis theirs] industries," which would not compete with local businesses. Article Six expressed the group's disapproval with the fact that "inhabitants whose property bordered on the waterfront have been deprived of the benefit of the beaches and their rights of access to the sea." Article Seven made the point that people with private jetties had never paid a poll tax that apparently was about to be imposed on them by the company. Article Eight asked that Wickham's Cay be supplied with its own water source. In the concluding article (Nine), the league noted that it "especially wished to record [its] disapproval of the clause whereby Wickham's Cay residents are to be exempt from taxes for ten years." It made the point that "we pay taxes and they must pay also since it is through taxes that the Government can be run."

The league's recommendations reveal its members' class background.[12] It clearly was concerned with the tax and property issues of the bourgeoisie, yet Articles Four and Five represent an embryonic nationalism that was in keeping with the league's other positions. The league was obviously determined to keep the financial rewards of development in the hands of Virgin Islanders.

Elite Virgin Islands men had been politicized early in the nineteenth century when they first demanded the right to vote on equal terms with white men. In the twentieth century, their politicization intensified with the creation of the Welfare Council in the 1930s. Since then, men had taken the leadership role in expressly political activities. They were also the ones chosen by the colonial authority to represent the colony at regional and extraregional conferences to determine the territory's political future.

The creation of the Community League by the wives of many of these politically active men signaled a politicization that stopped short of seeking office. The issues and concerns articulated by the league demonstrated the wide-ranging nature of its involvement in the society while contributing to a perception of women's new role in a new society.[13] League members wanted to shape the territory's *social* future. Clearly, they did not view their absence from the traditional and obvious sources of power, the Executive Council and the Legislative Council, as an impediment to their objectives. The fact that they did not, neither as a group nor as individuals, seek political office may indicate that as women of the elite, they had internalized and manifested a male dominance ideology to a greater degree than working-class women had. More likely though, their status gave them a degree of political access that the majority of women did not enjoy and eventually sought by running for office. Certainly, the league's sense of entitlement comes through in several of their documents. A letter written to the senior medical officer in May 1969 stated that "after a visit by some of our members, we came to the conclusion that an area adjoining the Infirmary should be cleared and levelled by a bulldozer to provide less hazardous terrain for use by the inmates. We, hereby, request that you use your influence to secure this operation by the Public Works Department."

The letter seems to be written by people who had every expectation that their requests would be honored. And the following resolution reads like one that could have been passed in the legislature. It says that the league "considers it expedient in the Public Interest that a Select Committee of the Legislative Council be appointed to receive local views and them make recommendations to the Government as to the future siting of the Public market and the Post Office."[14]

League members acted from a position of entitlement: they fully expected their concerns to be addressed by the government of the day.

This attitude is understandable given that at the time the above resolution likely was passed, the husband of President Marie O'Neal (Joseph R. O'Neal) was a nominated member of the government. Other members were in similarly influential positions. Emmogene Creque's husband (Henry O. Creque) was the Speaker of the House, and Norma Osborne's husband (Dr. Q. W. Osborne) was the leader of the BVI Democratic Party and the representative for District Five. The ability of the league's articulate and active members to shape government policy through their husbands should not be underestimated.

Though it is not clear exactly how many of the league's initiatives came to fruition, its representation on various private and public sector committees, its activities, and its submissions to government suggest that it did contribute to the shaping of Virgin Islands society at a turbulent time. Certainly its genteel and aristocratic but firm and assertive pursuit of members' interests demonstrated women's ability to play public roles. The league complemented the government's activities and supported its objectives. The government had decreed that tourism development was the means to the territory's prosperity, and the league embarked on an ambitious plan to clean and beautify the capital and to identify sites of potential historical interest to tourists. This symbiotic relationship was inevitable given the class and marital background of league members. But the league was equally enthusiastic about making its concerns about government policies known; hence, the questions concerning the secondary school and immigration regulations. It may not have promoted a women's rights agenda, but its members' easy assumption of a public role was the realization of a feminist vision of female empowerment.

WOMEN IN THE ECONOMY

The 1921 census reported that approximately 500 males were away in Cuba and Santo Domingo, out of a population of 5,082 people. Some of these men were accompanied by their wives. As they had in the 1800s, a large number of Virgin Islands women also went to the USVI on their own in search of work.[15] A College of the Virgin Islands report claimed that, by the 1960s, more than 1,400 alien women were working in private houses. (The number was higher still for men.) The majority of foreign workers came from Tortola, Jost Van Dyke, and Anegada. But problems were brewing.

An extract of a 1939 despatch records that

There used to be almost an entirely free flow of labour from Tortola . . . and that island . . . supplied much produce to the infertile and predominantly commercial island of St. Thomas. Gradually, however, the US Government has been tightening up immigration and commercial restrictions. Many British subjects in St. Thomas (except those who arrived before 1924) are technically illegal aliens and are liable to deportation.[16]

Immigration restrictions notwithstanding, many Virgin Islanders were able to enter and find work in the USVI, where wages were "very high and prices fair."[17] That they had to do so through "the back door" (illegally) in no way deterred their migration.

A BVI report stated that

Demand has led to a heavy migratory movement between the colony and St. Thomas and increased yet further the dependence of the colony on St. Thomas as the centre for paid employment. The extent of this demand and the effect upon the colony can be judged by the amount of passenger traffic between St. Thomas and Tortola and by the fact that in 1956 a total of over 900 persons, fully one-eighth of the population, had taken contract employment in St. Thomas as employees in hotels and private houses and as unskilled or semi-skilled workers.[18]

By the 1930s most of the land in the Virgin Islands was held by the people, but agriculture provided for little more than subsistence. A 1930 report declared that on Tortola alone there were 624 holdings of between 1 and 10 acres, 106 of 11 to 20 acres, and 23 of more than 100 acres. On Virgin Gorda, the third largest of the Virgins, there were 147 holdings of between 1 and 10 acres, 23 of between 11 and 20, and 2 of more than 100. The Agricultural Census of 1961 revealed 80 self-employed women involved in farming. Thirty-three had holdings of 1 acre or less, 21 had holdings of 5 acres or less, 18 had holdings of 10 acres or less, and 3 had holdings of 25 acres or less. Only 1 woman had more than 25 acres dedicated to agriculture. Four women had no land. The majority of the women were from the western side of Tortola (57), with 14 coming from East Tortola and 9 on Jost Van Dyke.[19] The fact that no women were recorded from Virgin Gorda and Anegada and that the numbers on Tortola were so small must lead to questions about how exactly the data was gathered and what the qualifications of a "farmer" were. Oral evidence that women provided a significant amount of agricultural labor throughout the twentieth century would seem to differ from the census data. "Every woman here had to go out and farm in order to survive," Jost Van Dyke farmer, Joyce Chinnery, points out.

Eadie wrote that "in Tortola it is the women who must work and their men who must watch and sleep" after seeing women on their way to market, the trays on their heads piled high with ground provisions. Although the observation may be an oversimplification, it stands to show women's continuing contribution to the economy.

The Moyne Commission noted that on the smaller islands "the inhabitants . . . show a most praiseworthy and attractive spirit of enterprise, independence and resource." In the Virgin Islanders this spirit was born of necessity. With no government of their own and little assistance from Britain, the people of the territory knew they could count only on themselves and each other.

To further their self-reliance, Virgin Islanders diversified their agricultural base so that they could be self-reliant and not have to depend on one main crop. The following excerpt from Eadie's book gives a descriptive account of the flourishing internal market in Road Town.

Gathered on the big square by the white wharf were crowds of natives who had tramped thither, balancing their wares upon their heads, over the rough mountain tracks from all parts of the island. There were no booths. The sellers mostly squatted on the ground with their produce in front of them in calabashes, in trays, or displayed on old sacking. Some had fixed up rough boards on trestles. Everyone appeared radiant as the sun and sea, exchanging the greetings of the market-place. Big Bella, the fish-wife was there in her spotted apron, fearlessly handling the many-coloured fish in their bristling armour. The women sellers wore picturesque white bandannas . . . some wore above the bandanna a ring of soft twisted material. These are called cottas—a name of African origin. A cotta helps to relieve the pressure and correct the balance of heavy weights upon the head. A few of the women flaunted crimson-hued bandannas. The men wore wide-brimmed sun-hats, woven of native rush, often artistically frayed at the edge. Some of the women also wore these sun-hats perched atop their bandannas.[20]

According to Eadie the produce on sale included "taniers [sic], sweet potatoes, yams, plantains, cho-chos or christophenes, squash, big yellow pumpkins . . . granadillas, soursops, sugar apples, native pawpaws, and wild sweet limes" and bananas. The "small patches" of land noted by Longden in the 1800s were still in full production. The people depended on them for their livelihood, thus maintaining a tradition centuries old.

Agricultural exports in the first half of the twentieth century included cotton lint, cattle, fruits and vegetables, small livestock, charcoal, dried fish, seed cotton, and fresh fish. Seventy-one-year-old farmer Ilva Lettsome recalls that her mother "used to supply St. John people. The boats would come over every Saturday and they would go with all her provisions and then she would send [some] over for who didn't come [to Tortola]." Women were making a significant contribution to the territory's export earnings. Idalia Parsons, sixty-nine, a farmer from New Bush, remembers that

The people who used to go to St. Thomas selling potatoes and tannias, they would come and buy them out from me. . . . They would come in at Brewer's Bay and that was where they used to take the cargo. Boats from Cane Garden Bay and boats from Carrot Bay. We didn't used to have very much for the market here because at that time we used to ship the things to St. Thomas.

In fact, women from all over the islands contributed to the trade with the American Virgin Islands. Jost Van Dyke farmer Olivia Callwood, eighty-six, noted that her family "used to send the largest we had to St. Thomas, goats and cows and pigs."

Levo noted that St. Thomas ate what Tortola grew. Canoes and sloops set sail from the BVI usually on a Monday morning, loaded with small livestock, cattle, fruits, and vegetables. St. Thomas residents would crowd what became known as Tortola Wharf in Charlotte Amalie to purchase that week's requirements, inquire about relatives, receive gift packages, and hear the latest news. When there was more produce than buyers, the boatmen would put pans of potatoes, bunches of bananas, and other produce on their heads and go into the alleys, hawking their goods.

Livestock and fresh produce weren't the only commodities exported by Virgin Islands women. "I custom burning coal . . . We used to cut the wood from till back of the hill out yonder and send the coal St. Thomas by boat and sell them," says Violet Stevens, eighty, who has farmed on Virgin Gorda most of her life. Women's involvement in coal production was extensive.

Christalia Hodge recollects burning coal with her mother. "We would cut the wood. Any kind of wood. Throw them into the coal pit dock today. Tomorrow you set up your coal pit. You light it the third day and as fast as it burn you haul it. The coal would be sold at market. Every week we would burn a coal pit in time for market."

The coal was produced for home consumption, for sale on and between the different Virgin Islands, and for export. Eileene Parsons, who grew up in St. Thomas and whose mother and grandmother were farmers, remembers the importance of coal from Tortola to the St. Thomas market. "Stoves were something rarely seen [before the 1960s] and the few stoves were kerosene, you would now say paraffin. There was no gas, it was unknown. Coal was the order of the day and the coal came from Tortola. Boats used to go down loaded with nothing but coal. In St. Thomas, young boys or men from here would hawk coal through the streets."

In 1941, exported livestock (horses, mules, goats, and sheep) brought in approximately £14,000 to the small territory but large-scale agriculture was declining. Sea Island cotton, introduced into the islands in the early 1900s, had fallen from 210 acres under cultivation in 1939 to 83 acres in 1941. The efforts of the Experimental Station of the Agricultural Department to encourage farmers toward the production of cotton, sugar, and tobacco, all labor-intensive crops, had failed. Colonial officials blamed the decline on "migration, the adoption of culture patterns of urban St. Thomas, competition from cheap, mass-produced, fresh and processed American foods, partial loss of the St. Thomas market and lack of marketing organisation."[21]

Another cause, apparently unrecognized, was that women's role in agriculture had been ignored. Even if they received funds and assistance from the Experimental Station, the emphasis on large-scale agriculture ignored women's deep involvement in the production and marketing of ground provisions and vegetables and the raising of livestock. The agricultural industry, then the pillar of the Virgin Islands economy, rested on stock breeding and on the production of ground provisions, vegetables, and fruits. In 1960, approximately 700 acres of Crown land was rented to farmers. Ilva Lettsome's mother alone grew tomatoes, peas, cabbages, eggplants, potatoes, and bananas. Idalia Parsons remembers her mother growing a similar variety. "In the years past we grow everything, sweet potato, tannias, bananas, pineapples, papaya." By 1956, sweet potatoes and bananas were the two principal cash or export crops.

Eggleston related the story of Princess Alexandrine, a Jost Van Dyke woman, whose husband had died around the turn of the century and left her with nine children and "a couple of head of cattle."

Starting from there she got her little store going and acquired a few more cattle. She managed to bring up all the children and see them through such schooling as was available. Her livestock grew until she now owns most of the cattle on Jost Van

Dyke. She also owns Little Tobago Island and leases it to a man who is raising goats there.

Yet the Department of Agriculture appeared to ignore these women's industry, making no special concessions to the nature of their work and the obstacles they, in particular, may have faced.

Agricultural work was not the only work available to women.

In the early 1950s, businesspeople in St. Thomas initiated the production of a cologne for men based on the bay rum plant found in profusion throughout the Virgin Islands. An East End man, Ebert Lettsome, became the local agent and brought cases of the cologne to East End, Tortola, every two weeks. The cases were then distributed among women in the community who knit straw jackets for the bottles. "A woman would go to Mr. Lettsome's house to be assigned her work. Cases contained four, eight or 16 ounce sizes of 36 or 48 bottles. If she was a fast and competent craftswoman, she would have two or three cases. She would also buy her straw [from Mr. Lettsome] and receive about $6.00 for each four ounce case she had done, $8.00 for each eight ounce case and $10. for each 16 ounce case."[22]

The work required high skill levels. The women first had to "set up the bottles" or prepare the "fish-eye" pattern on her work table, then frame the bottles or fit the matting to the bottles. The last task was "trimming the bottles" to remove all protruding ends. Women were still working for the Bay Rum company in 1990.

Another industry begun in the mid-1950s was the Gustave Slipper Factory, which started operating in Road Town. Eileene Parsons, who was asked to teach crochet to the women employed by Gustave and who ended up managing the factory, recalls how it got started and how it functioned:

Mr. Gustave was going to open in St. Thomas but Mr. Lindquist, a gentleman from St. Thomas, who happened to be a friend of Mr. Howard Penn, he came over here and got Mr. Penn interested. Government got interested and they said they would do a pilot project. Then it was a matter of finding somebody who could teach persons to crochet. I was already out of high school and not only could I crochet but I had a certain level of education [and] I could crochet by reading the directions [so I was hired]. We started with about twenty, thirty women and it kept going up. I know it was more than one hundred. He would send the raw materials over here, the soles of the shoes, the spools of thread. I had taught most of the women to crochet and they would crochet and lock the shoe on and then we started giving them the shoes to take home as piece work. It was suggested they not be given more than a dozen pairs but since I was in charge and the women lived out in the country I would give them two, three bags. A bag had a dozen. I'd learned that a lot of them had taught their husbands how to do it. It was really difficult work to lock the sole on the shoe, you had to push the crochet hook under. I was told that a lot of women taught their husbands how to lay the straw, how to lock. It was a family thing. The women would crochet the little gold or silver tops and the husband would lock them unto the sole and finish them and the women would bring them in. The women were paid by the pair.

By the end of the first year (1953), 3,500 pairs of slippers had been produced. By the second year, production had more than quadrupled, rising to 15,774. The shoes were packed for shipment to St. Thomas every Friday and Saturday, then shipped out on Monday mornings. In St. Thomas they would be bought for between six and ten dollars a pair.

In 1955, however, the factory shut down regular operations because of "tariff difficulties in marketing in the United States."[23] The tax on each pair of shoes had started out at 3 percent, but it went up to 6 percent a pair. Though efforts were made to seek other markets in Europe, these were unsuccessful, and the factory soon ceased operations in the Virgin Islands.[24] For the few years in which it operated, the factory was the single largest employer of women in the territory and had a significant impact on women's earning ability. Some were able to buy land from their factory wages. Parsons comments on this:

I could only talk about some I know in the Fahie Hill area. A lady named Mrs. Emmy Smith there, her family had land up in Fahie Hill and [they] wanted to sell. They divided that land in quarter acres and I know three women [from the Factory who bought that land]. It was sold then at $72 for a quarter acre. An aunt of mine, my sister, a lady, Louise Scatliffe, they also bought land from their earnings at Gustave. It was a solid income for those women and their families.[25]

That these women often chose to purchase land reinforces theories of women's identification with the land as their basis for citizenship. In buying land, these women laid claim to the country of their birth. Their jobs at Gustave had given them a financial freedom that they may not have found elsewhere. The factory allowed them to participate in the long tradition of Virgin Islands women who were capable breadwinners. More than that, it gave them the chance to leave behind a tangible legacy for their children.

As the Virgin Islands changed and prospered, the huckstering tradition in which many women had participated persisted. Anna Augusta Malone remembers assisting her aunt Fanny in bread baking. After the bread was ready, Malone would put a basket of bread on her head and take it around the neighborhood to sell just like Ariange had in the previous century. But huckstering gradually gave way to shopkeeping. Women-owned shops sprang up throughout the territory.

In Fahie Hill, I remember Catherine Malone. Also there was . . . her name was Florence, but they called her Madam Buckley, she kept shop, baked bread and so forth. Another was Catherine Todman, she mostly sold oil and matches. Down in town I remember Miss Jane Horton. Emmogene Creque also had a shop. Up the town, Miss Baby Georges, she mostly sold bread and up the head of the town, Miss Kate, I think she used to sell bread, and puddings and that sort of thing. Over Baugher's

Bay, Miss Florie, Miss Florie Pickering. Almost all the stores in the different communities were owned by women. Up in our area it was the staples, flour, sugar, matches, rice, fats, sweet oil, butter lard, that sort of thing. Fabrics and shoes and hats were sold in town.[26]

Some of these women were single, the spinsters of their communities who were basically free to do as they wanted when it came to business enterprise, a boast their married sisters could not always make. By starting their own businesses, married women demonstrated their disinterest in being simply incorporated wives who remained in the background of their husbands' public lives. This wasn't always appreciated. In the mid-1930s when Emmogene Creque decided to go into business selling dry goods and groceries, her husband attempted to dissuade her from the venture, citing the difficulties involved.

Among other things she had to travel to St. Thomas by sailing boat to meet sales agents from whom she made purchases. The difficulties she faced not only entailed the physical stress of travel, but also homemaking and managing the finances. Her husband encouraged her to abandon what he thought was a difficult venture, one that was onerous, one which could well turn out to be unprofitable. These efforts . . . were firmly resisted. [The] business continues today.[27]

Other women shop owners on Tortola have included Zephera Smith, Reubena Akiel, and Alice Henley. These women, though they may not have known it, were the clear inheritors of black women's huckstering legacy described in previous chapters. In fact, their ability to carry on successful businesses may very well have depended on the pioneering industry of women such as Christiana Wheatley and others. Certainly the work of the hucksters, building on women's marketing customs established in Africa, accustomed the society to the concept of women's entrepreneurial undertakings.

Following the recommendations of various consultants, the government on Tortola decided to promote the development of Virgin Islands agriculture and to encourage tourism.[28] New markets for agricultural products were sought, and in 1953, the Hotel Aid Ordinance was passed. Colonial officials began to be optimistic about the territory's progress. "The general atmosphere in the Presidency is better than for many years past. This is due in part to reasonable prosperity resulting from the sale of cattle at good prices to the French islands and in part to the fact that excellent progress has at long last been made with the execution of a number of development projects."[29]

Outward migration began to taper off. In 1956, seventy-five men were contracted from the territory to work as cane cutters in St. Croix, but by 1960 that number had dropped to eight. A year later, 130 Virgin Islanders were employed at Little Dix Bay, the new resort owned by Laurence

Rockefeller on Virgin Gorda.[30] With the opening of Little Dix, the Virgin Islands entered a new era in which agriculture, and particularly large-scale agriculture, became less and less important. Both men and women flocked to the service economy, finding there a high-paying alternative to migration. The move proved ambiguous for women, however. The decline of the sugar plantations in the 1800s and the subsequent failure to substitute cotton and tobacco had resulted in a heavy reliance on women's work in the production of vegetables, fruits, and ground provisions. Because men also worked their grounds and sometimes sold in the markets along with the fishermen, the line dividing the contributions made by the two sexes to the economy remained somewhat blurred. But the introduction of the hotel industry intensified the distinctions.

The development of a service economy coincided with an explosive growth in the civil service. Both of these sectors encouraged and developed an environment in which gender roles diverged sharply. George Lamming has labeled the tourism industry in the Caribbean "Plantation Phase II."[31] Although he may have been referring to racial issues, his comment applies equally to gender. Though women were the equals of men in the sugar fields, many of the skilled jobs on the plantation, such as those connected with the factory, were reserved for men. Similarly, the advent of the service economy saw women performing low-paying domestic and secretarial work while men entered the skilled professions and middle and upper management. The accompanying encroachment of patriarchal ideology meant that many had no problem with this. In a 1961 letter to the editor of *The Tortola Times*, one woman, herself a prominent Road Town merchant, wrote that she liked "to see not only our girls but to a greater extent our boys excel."[32] Men had taken the lead in the political leadership of the territory, and this was seen as natural, an inevitable devolution of colonial authority that had always been masculine. Women were not part of nor party to the contract made between local male policy shapers and foreign male policy makers. Their attempts to break the political mold or to ascend the government hierarchy to a position where they too could influence public policy in a direct way were seen as attempts to usurp the male role. Women's advancement was thus met with resistance and hostility. As we shall see later, this had dire consequences for the possibility of women's electoral success.

WOMEN IN EDUCATION: LEADING THE WAY

The history of education in the Virgin Islands is really the history of women's contributions and achievements in this sector. As has been noted in previous chapters, schools in the territory were organized by the churches and received supplemental funds from the government. Most of the teachers were women. The Numerical Return of Synod Day Schools in

1912 records seven schools on Tortola and a teaching staff of five men and seven women. The number of Methodist elementary day schools had risen to eight in 1929. By that time there were six male and fifteen female teachers. The schools were small, attendance fluctuated, and teachers concentrated on the basics: reading, writing, arithmetic, and the scriptures. With the passage of the Elementary Education Act in 1925, the colonial authorities expanded the curriculum to include history and geography. The following year, the Leeward Islands Legislative Council passed a law that provided for the creation of a Board of Education to appoint teachers, the extension of compulsory education from twelve to fifteen years, and the reorganization of schools into three divisions. At this time the pupil-teacher system was in operation. (Pupil teachers were recent graduates.) A report on conditions in the Virgin Islands explained that "studentships [were] awarded to specially selected candidates, at the conclusion of their pupil teachership, [usually after three years] for two years to complete their training as assistant teachers. Those for girls are held at the Spring Gardens Teachers Training College in Antigua."[33]

In 1936, a Teacher's Association was formed. At that time there were approximately seven male and eighteen female teachers in the nine day schools operated by the Methodists. The demand for education was growing. Parents who themselves had not attended much school were determined that their children would. "My children went to school . . . they never do no farming," says Idalia Parsons. Many parents chose to forgo their children's help on the farm in favor of their education. Olivia Callwood's fourteen children all went to school instead of assisting their parents. "They had to go to school . . . I couldn't afford them not to," she says.

In 1942, the Department of Education was established. At the time the Virgin Islands had eleven schools, two of which were run by the Anglican Church and the rest by the Methodists.

Following in the footsteps of women such as Grace Frett, some women started their own schools independent of the churches. In 1902, at the age of eighteen, Leonora Delville opened a school at West End. Like the other schools operating in the territory, this was probably an all-age school for children ranging from five to twelve and possibly above. Though her reason for opening the school is not given in the brief biography available, it is reasonable to assume that it was for the same reason she reopened it years later—out of concern for the distance children at the western end of the island had to travel to get to school. Twenty years later the school closed and Delville entered the public school system and taught at the Upper Zion Hill Church. When the church was destroyed in the 1924 hurricane, she resigned from the teaching service and did not reenter it until 1950. The territory was then just beginning to enter the modern era, but children still had to travel great distances to attend school. Once again Delville's school operated out of her residence. Many of the children's parents were unable to pay her monthly fees of between four and ten dollars, but Delville was willing to overlook nonpayment.

In the 1940s, Alexandrina Frett-Maduro started a school out of her house in Baugher's Bay. Frett-Maduro had previously taught at the East End Village School but had relocated to Baugher's Bay after her marriage. When she moved the school to a rented building, it became known as the Baugher's Bay Community School. (The government later took it over and renamed it in her honor in 1981.)

By 1970 there were

Six private unaided schools and three others, each of which received a small grant as a Community School. The enrolment of the unaided private schools is 225 (104 boys and 121 girls) between the ages of 2 and 11. They serve a useful purpose in providing education below the normal age of entry to the Government's primary schools and depend entirely on fees to pay salaries and overhead costs. Only one private school, that in Carrot Bay, has both primary and post-primary sections. One school which has an infant section offers training in typing to a few adult students.[34]

Earlier, the Moyne Commission had observed that "few administrative posts are held by West Indian women who are employed in the Civil Service mainly as teachers or clerks, etc., and in Postal Departments." Of the eighteen teachers in the colony in 1942, eleven were women; six of the eleven pupil teachers also were women. A head teacher then made about £12 per year and an assistant teacher £9. Salaries for teachers in the Virgin Islands were, according to Wakefield, the education commissioner, "the lowest in the Windward and Leeward Islands," a fact that could explain the absence of men. In addition, many women teachers suffered extreme hardship in pursuit of their chosen profession. One woman recalls that in the thirties and forties, she and her horse sometimes had to swim through ponds and ghuts to get to and from wherever she was teaching. Another teacher, Althea Scatliffe, was transferred to teach on Anegada in the late 1920s, a time when the trip to the most northerly of the Virgin Islands took a minimum of five hours by sailboat. There was no jetty, so on arrival, passengers were often carried ashore by the crew. From stories like that, one senses that teaching was more than a profession to these women.[35] Their dedication indicates that they felt themselves to be performing a critical role in the development of their country. It was almost solely due to their efforts that in the 1946 census of the four Leeward Island presidencies, the Virgin Islands had the highest ratio of literate people to the total population. Sixty-nine percent were able to read, and 86 percent of those aged ten and over could both read and write.

Near the middle of the century, the territory's advancement demanded the establishment of a secondary school. Over the objections of the education commissioner, the V. I. Senior School was opened in 1943.[36] Four of the staff of seven were women. Women taught domestic science, hygiene and physiology, religious education, language, and literature, and men taught math, botany, woodwork, and geography.

Education Commissioner Wakefield, faced with the creation of a secondary school over his objections, devoted his energies to ensuring the engendering of patriarchal norms among both students and teachers. He wrote that

The essence of the homecraft needed in the Virgin Islands is the proper care of children and in practise this involves most of the basic lessons of housework, laundering, needlework, and the clean preparation of food with a better focus (upon living infants) and a more natural and stronger motive power in girls (their awakening maternal feelings) than is found in the ordinary teaching of domestic science.[37]

Wakefield recommended the creation of a play center on the school's grounds that would act as a "practical laboratory of housecraft." This enthusiasm reveals much about the commissioner's dedication to perpetuating, if not enhancing, the status quo. Obviously, in his view, education for women mattered little if it did not prepare them for their roles as wives and mothers. Earlier the Moyne Commission had warned that "if there are to be happy marriages girls must be able to be companions to their husbands and therefore need every opportunity for as wide a cultural education as possible." The commission made haste to affirm, however, that "domestic science should, of course, form a part of the curriculum in all girls' schools." Colonial authorities obviously agreed that girls should be trained for successful wifedom, but they differed on how exactly this was to be achieved.

In the nineteenth century, colonial officials were concerned that the education provided to the freed blacks inculcate the values of hard work, obedience, and respect for the empire. What was asked of women in the twentieth century was essentially the same thing, but being as removed as they were from governance or the state, their obedience and respect was to be directed to the men in their lives. Women were expected to be loyal subjects too, but in their case they were to show their loyalty by serving their men and through them, the state.[38]

Colonialism and patriarchy thus formed an intersecting web of interests and prejudices in which the image of black men loyal to monarch and empire was as cherished as the image of maternal (and submissive) Virgin Islands women. The fact that the education system had for so long been under the domination of the church contributed greatly to the dissemination of ideas relating to the appropriateness of women's subjection to men. Still, education itself was the best way to secure advancement, and women continued to participate in that sector in high numbers, causing much alarm in certain circles.

In 1949, an editorial in *The Torch* bewailed the ratio of boys to girls in the schools:

At the moment there are ten or eleven boys in the Virgin Islands High School. It would appear that leadership will be confined exclusively, or at least very largely, to women. This is a situation that requires serious consideration. It is not as if the boys are non-existent. They are here but are they being [given] their chance?

Even those of us without sons could possibly use our influence to secure that a greater number of men are prepared for the important job of leadership.

At the time, *The Torch's* publisher, the Virgin Islands Welfare Committee, was vigorously promoting the concept of greater internal self-rule. Education was the route to the economic and political power so long denied Virgin Islanders; if boys were absent from the classroom, then in time, men would be absent from government. The thought that they were agitating for greater power only to see it fall into women's hands obviously worried the council's all-male membership.

Statistics supported the council's observation about women's high participation in education. A 1961 report found that by post-primary, the number of boys attending school had dropped from 928 to 137, whereas that of girls went from 873 to 180.[39] Though there were steep declines for both sexes, boys went from being in the majority to being in the minority. In 1959, there were 80 girls in the secondary school but only 25 boys. In 1961, 82 girls attended secondary school but only 37 boys.[40] The report further noted that out of the 70 teachers at the primary school level, 55 were women who were more likely than their male colleagues to have completed a secondary school course.[41] Those numbers remained near constant for years. In 1964 it was reported that girls constituted 49 percent of primary school attendees and 70 percent of attendees at the secondary school. That year the number of female primary school teachers had increased to 59, whereas the number of males had dropped to 13; in the secondary school, there were five female and five male teachers.

As was pointed out earlier, many of these teachers gained exposure to education methods by attending the Spring Gardens Teacher's Training College in Antigua. Discussions under the Inter-VI Conference also led, in 1959, to plans for teachers from the Virgin Islands to attend the Hampton Institute Summer Courses held in St. Croix.[42] Women teachers' education, combined with their experiences abroad, set the groundwork for their advancement not only in the field of education but also in the society at large as will be demonstrated in following chapters.

Even with the widening of the economic base in the 1970s and 1980s (when the tourism and finance industries were introduced into the territory), many women saw (and continue to see) teaching as a stepping-stone to other public careers. In 1960, *The Tortola Times* carried a brief article on a woman who had won the Hampton Award for outstanding work in teaching. The award provided a five-week course at the University of the West Indies. There is also the example of Enid Leona Scatliffe, who won a Leeward Islands Scholarship in 1939 and enrolled in the Spring Gardens

Teacher's Training College in Antigua. From there she went to the Government Training College in Trinidad in 1943. In 1959, she was appointed to the staff of the education department as supervising teacher. Fifteen years later Scatliffe became the first woman appointed to the post of chief education officer, which she held for six years.

These women and others like them also represented the territory at subregional and regional teacher conferences. The status gained by their time and experience in other countries lent them an enhanced authority that the fact of their sex would not have been able to obtain. Of course teaching itself provided them with status. Seven of the twelve schools in the territory that have been named after deserving educators have been named after women.

WOMEN IN HEALTH

As they had during slavery and afterward, many women continued to act as traditional healers. Cupping was a way of relieving aches and pains caused by a blow. A small cut was made in the bruised area, which was "cupped" by a small calabash dampened with rum. The calabash was then lit, and the suction created drew off the congested blood. Jane Eliza Henley was one woman to whom many went for this type of healing. Other healers such as Caroline "Tonco" Henley used leeches to draw off blood from inflamed areas. And many women continued to use medicinal plants for a wide range of purposes, from easing headaches to relieving pain to "cleansing the blood." They were the "bush doctors" who could trace their knowledge of healing plants to their slave ancestors. They, along with the bone setters, were the only "doctors" many Virgin Islanders, particularly those in the country areas and the sister islands, ever saw.

Midwives also played an important role in Virgin Islands society, but they weren't universally appreciated. In the 1920s, the sole doctor in the territory, Dr. Wailing, bemoaned the dependence of the local population on "native midwives who have had no training and have learned a little by experience." There is no previous evidence of any dissatisfaction on the doctors' part with midwives. Given the distances doctors had to travel from their base in Road Town, the midwives' assistance was highly valued by the communities they served. In fact, Trevor notes that the midwife "who delivers a child's mother is known as its 'grannie.'" Midwives were thus perceived to have a familial bond with the children they helped bring into the world. In the first few days after the birth, the midwife was seen as indispensable. "The midwife visits the mother daily and washes the infant until its "navel string" or umbilical cord—three times the length of the midwife's middle finger—falls off which may be from five days to a week after birth."

Until the present time, these community-based midwives, inheritors of a legacy with its roots in slavery and beyond, are fondly remembered. Eileene Parsons recalled midwives she's known:

My grandmother, Pinky, was a midwife and Muddy delivered an untold number of children. And then there was Christiana, she was a middy. I think Penny Donovan's grandmother, she was a midwife. I know they would go at any time. You call them at midnight and they would go to deliver a baby. I know in West End there was one living at the Towers. I don't know her first name but we used to call her Friend Dodie. She would go all over Carrot Bay until the government started the district nursing system.

A brief account of another midwife, Catherine "Katie Ben" Parrot, gives an idea of just how extensive their services were to the community.

Katie served the Belle Vue, Cooten Bay, Long Trench, Fahie Hill areas for many in the 1920s to the early 1940s. In addition to the women of the area, she was the "granny" who brought her daughters and granddaughters "to bed" at the time of their "lying in." At the time of her death on April 19th, 1945 at the age of 71 she had acted as "granny" at the birth of over 70 plus grandchildren, which included several sets of twins, and great grandchildren.[43]

The reach and influence of the midwives was clearly considerable, but their heydays were numbered. With Governor H. W. Peebles's administration of the Leeward Islands had come some changes. In 1922, a two-room hospital was built in Road Town that acquired a small nursing staff of an English matron and two local nurses. The Virgin Islands were undergoing a period of modernization.[44] Science was seen as the light that would guide the locals out of the darkness of traditional customs and practices. Midwifery was one of those customs and practices expected to give way. Dr. Wailing quite likely viewed reliance on midwives as a threat to his authority, both as doctor and, later, as commissioner. His pride affronted, he embarked on an energetic campaign to break the influence of the midwives and to encourage expecting women to deliver at the new hospital. "I am trying to persuade others to attend [the hospital] but without success," Wailing lamented in 1927. A few years later the Executive Council dismissed a proposal to train the midwives and, instead, the effort to persuade pregnant women to give birth in the hospital intensified.[45] With the weight of science and masculine colonial authority against the midwives, the battle began to turn. By 1935 the medical officer could report that "no persuasion is necessary to get the mothers into hospital where they are sure of the best attention and every comfort." Though the doctor mentions cases of women riding in from as much as five miles away and later suffering ante-partum hemorrhage, his confidence in the superiority of hospital care was apparently unshaken. These women were essentially the casualties in the power struggle between the doctor and the midwives, a battle he began.

Though many more women were coming in to the hospital, some continued to rely on the midwives who probably had been present at their own births. "Peebles Hospital had come but there were women up [in the country] who still didn't trust what they called 'the little girls by the hospital,'" Parsons remembers. The 1942 medical report claims that "two hundred and forty-nine expectant mothers attended for ante-natal care," but the fact that there were only forty deliveries at the hospital suggests that midwives had not disappeared completely. At the time the hospital consisted only of a five-bed male ward, a five-bed female ward, and a single private bed.

The eventual decline of midwives was accompanied by a rise in the importance of nurses. Of course the nurses received official sanction from male colonial authority as represented by the health officer and, ultimately, the commissioner. Midwives, on the other hand, had earned their status through apprenticeship with other women. They practiced as equals who were unconnected by any established hierarchical or associative system. By effecting their decline, the doctor established a health care network with him, the masculine authority, at the top. Co-opting women, who, as sanctioned nurses, would undermine the authority of the midwives while being subservient to him, was a bold blow against a vital source of women's power in their communities.

But breaking the influence of midwives was a slow process hampered by the need to train local nurses and the geography of the islands. In 1927, the annual medical report noted that there were two local nurses on the medical staff, both of whom were undergoing training. According to that report, their duties consisted primarily of "seeing that patients are provided with the food prescribed at proper and regular hours."[46] The nurses worked long hours. Adina Donovan recalls that "two of us had day duty for about ten hours and one night duty for twelve hours. We had every other Sunday off after certain chores had been completed in the morning." A nurse's salary was then about nine dollars per month.

By the late 1930s, the poverty of the territory's finances persuaded the colonial authorities to replace the European matron at the hospital with a West Indian nurse.[47] The matron acted as dispenser in charge of drugs and dressings, was responsible for the order and discipline of staff, and was in charge of bedding, clothing, and so on.

In 1940, Wailing, then the commissioner, decided to establish a system of district nurses on the major sister islands and in Tortola's countryside. At first the plan did not meet with "the success hoped for" on the sister islands. Wailing attributed the failure to the islands' remote loneliness. He decided that "the only solution is to train girls from these islands who would be content to live and work in their own homes." By 1942 there were seven district nurses throughout the colony. They were responsible for "minor medical treatment especially for women and children, visiting the sick at home, midwifery (pre- and post-natal services), school nursing and so on." Each nurse was responsible for an average of 200 families.

The creation of the district nursing system was but one sign of the burgeoning health sector. The Virgin Islands entered the twentieth century with one doctor as the only person on the medical staff, but by 1965, the islands had a staff of twenty-two health personnel, only five of whom were male. The gains made by women in the health field were ambiguous, however, given their initial positioning on the lowest rungs of the medical hierarchy. Except for the matron, the seventeen women in the health system were all nurses with little status within the system itself. Indeed, even the matron's status was diminished somewhat with the reduction in her responsibilities entailed by the appointment of a male dispenser in the early 1940s. In the community, however, where doctor visits were relatively rare, the standing of the nurses would have been high. For many, a nurse was the first and only member of the health staff patients saw, and for others she was the intermediary who made their appointments with the doctor possible.

NOTES

1. Quoted in Karen Tranberg-Hansen, "White Women in a Changing World: Employment, Voluntary Work and Sex in Post World War II Northern Rhodesia," in *Western Women and Imperialism: Complicity and Resistance,* ed. Naipur Chaudhuri and Margaret Strobel (Bloomington: Indiana University Press, 1992), pp. 247–268.

2. French believes that "the introduction of Women's Institutes to the West Indies had the official support of the British government and . . . [was] the result of an official initiative." Joan French, *Women and Colonial Policy after the 1938 Uprising in Jamaica* (Kingston: University of the West Indies, 1989), 121–143. For more on colonial policy toward women see *West India Royal Commission [or Moyne] Report* (London: HMSO, 1945), p. 217.

3. Plaits or woven straw was used to make the hats and bags.

4. Interview by author with Eugenie Todman-Smith, September 1998, Road Town.

5. Ivan Dawson, *A Brief Outline of a Humble Life* (Tortola: Ivan Dawson, 1993), p. 29.

6. S. A. Hammond, *Leeward Islands Report on an Enquiry Into the Organization and Salaries of the Civil Service* (London: Her Majesty's Stationery Office, 1952), p. 154.

7. The civil service would have taken a backward step if it had followed Hammond's suggestion that "women holding pensionable office should be required to resign upon marriage." He tried to sweeten the pill by recommending that women who had given five or more pensionable years of service should be given a marriage gratuity and be eligible for employment on a monthly basis. Hammond, p. 155. According to him, "a colony in the financial position of the Leeward Islands . . . cannot afford to employ persons who are absent for long periods [on maternity leave] in addition to their normal leave entitlement." Hammond, p. 155.

8. Though the size of the territory could have been expected to preclude distinctions between town and country, those distinctions were very much in effect. Town residents were considered and considered themselves the elite. Several factors contributed to this perception. The standard of education offered at the Road Town school was superior to that given in country schools. Country people were not officially excluded from going to school in town, but the physical difficulties posed by traveling hilly paths or the economic difficulties of boarding children in town precluded most from making the attempt. Educated town residents had the edge in business dealings and appointments to the civil service. Townspeople were generally better off, and most were not involved in agriculture, which stigmatized country people further. As the seat of government, Road Town was also the most highly developed. Paved roads, electricity, and communications services were offered first in Road Town before being diffused throughout the territory. Townspeople therefore considered themselves more sophisticated than those from the country.

9. Letter to Chief Minister, 9 March 1968, BVI Community League.

10. The college was run by British women expatriates. In 1919, Florence Thomas became the first local woman to enroll in the women-only school.

11. In the 1970s, 669 women and 617 men migrated to the colony. Raymond Phillips, *1980–1991 Population and Housing Census of the Commonwealth Caribbean: National Census Report, British Virgin Islands* (Guyana: Caricom, 1992), p. 9.

12. Article Seven questions why a poll tax should be paid to dock at the proposed marina "when our beaches were taken from us without our knowledge and permission." BV Community League Memorandum, 18 September 1969.

13. On learning of the assassination of Martin Luther King Jr. in the United States, the league sent a letter to the chief minister suggesting that flags be flown at half-mast throughout the territory on the day of the funeral. The league also recommended sending a condolence message to Dr. King's wife and broadcasting a special program eulogizing him. Letter from BVI Community League to Chief Minister, 10 April 1968.

14. Though it is unclear when this resolution was passed, it is likely to have been in the first half of 1968, as minutes recorded at meetings in those months mention the league's concern about the market and post office. Notes in possession of Linda O'Neal.

15. Although Virgin Islanders had always found work in the USVI, the construction of military bases on St. Thomas and St. Croix during World War II significantly increased the demand for labor. *The Alien Worker and His family* (conference proceedings). (Charlotte Amalie: College of the Virgin Islands, 1967), p. 5.

16. Extract of a despatch for Inspector General Maclean. 10 July 1939. *CO 318/436/14.*

17. Report by Governor G. Gordon Lethem to the Secretary of State for the Colonies. 23 July 1936. *CO 152/465/16.*

18. *Report of the BVI, 1955 and 1956* (London: HMSO, 1956), p. 6.

19. According to the census, the paid agricultural workers in the Virgin Islands (153) were all male.

20. Hazel Balance Eadie, *Lagooned in the Virgin Islands* (London: George Routledge and Sons, 1931), pp. 49–50.

21. *BVI Report, 1955 and 1956*, p. 19.

22. Ermin Burnett, "The Bottle Industry," in *Virgin Islands Historical Documents* 3, 1 (May 1990). Library Services Department, Ministry of Health, Education and Welfare, p. 3.

23. *BVI Report 1955 and 1956*, p. 26.

24. According to Parsons, Gustave also had a factory in Puerto Rico where he could make the slippers for less and from which he could ship them to the United States without paying customs duties.

25. Interview by author with Eileene Parsons, 12 August 1998, Road Town.

26. Ibid.

27. Biography of Emmogene Creque, in *Women in the Legislative Council* (Virgin Islands: The Women's Desk, Office of the Chief Minister, 1997), pp. 7–8.

28. These included Dr. Carleen O'Laughlin's 1962 "Survey of the Economic Potential, Fiscal Structure and Capital Requirements of the British Virgin Islands" and Dr. William Phillips's 1966 "Report on the British Virgin Islands with Recommendations on Measures for Accelerating Economic and Social Development." Dr. O'Laughlin was a professor at the University of the West Indies, and Dr. Phillips was a United Nations economic adviser.

29. Political Report, January 1954. *CO 1031/1811*. From 1953 to 1956, Martinique was the chief market for local cattle.

30. Political Report, September 1961. *CO 1031/3743*. The Hotel Aid Ordinance signaled the arrival of what Spackman calls "industrialization by invitation: the direct encouragement of further foreign control over the separate economies of the territory." In the interest of this economic colonization, political leaders concluded that political colonization had to continue, that the British flag encourages foreign investment and should not be lowered.

31. Quoted in Linda Banks-Devonish and Phyllis Flemming-Banks, *National Report on the Status of Women in the British Virgin Islands* (Road Town: Women's Desk, 1994), p. 7.

32. The letter writer, Reubena Akiel, owner of Ruby's Fancy Department Store, was commenting on the appointments of two men to senior posts in the civil service. *Tortola Times*, 21 January 1961, p. 3.

33. Annual General Report for the Leeward Islands, 1927–1928. *CO 152/408/19*.

34. *BVI Report, 1970* (London: HMSO, 1970), pp. 19–20.

35. Of course, many of these women themselves had to travel great distances as schoolchildren. As a girl, Althea Scatliffe walked every day from her home in Helmsley, on the road to Brewer's Bay, to the Methodist School in Road Town. (BVI: Department of Education Calendar, 1996.) On a map the distance does not seem far, but the walk would have involved traveling over hilly terrain at a time when no paved roads existed in the territory. The walk could have easily taken more than two hours each way.

36. In 1942, Commissioner of Education Wakefield wrote to Jardine that there was "at present time no justification for founding [a senior secondary school]." *CO 318/451/9.*

37. Wakefield Report, 1942. *CO 318/451/9.*

38. According to Varlack and Harrigan, boys were taught history and geography "with special reference to the Empire and the Union Jack," but girls received instruction in needlework and crafts.

39. BVI Administrator's Reports, Education Report, 1961. *CO 316/19.* The reorganization of the school system in the early 1960s had resulted in the disappearance of the all-age schools. Instead, the primary schools offered five years of education, after which the majority of students went into the three-year post-primary program.

40. BVI Administrator's Reports, Education Report, 1961. *CO 316/19.* The most promising students went to the secondary school, which was then known as the Senior or Grammar School and was in Road Town. It offered a five-year program, at the end of which students sat the Cambridge School Certificate of Education examinations.

41. There were five male teachers as opposed to four female in the secondary school. Education Report, 1961. *CO 316/19.*

42. "Teacher to Attend Summer Course," *Tortola Times,* 18 July 1959. The first nominee to do so was Inez Turnbull, head teacher of the Cane Garden Bay School, who had been trained at Spring Gardens.

43. "Midwives and the Grannies," in *150 Years of Achievement, 1834–1984.* (BVI: Department of Education, 1934), p. 21.

44. The modernization trend was most notable in agriculture. In 1900, the Imperial Agriculture Department established an experiment station and hired an agricultural instructor to disseminate new methods of cultivation.

45. The proposal was brought by Dr. Joynt, who had recently joined the medical staff. Executive Council Minutes, 20 February 1930. *CO 316/12.*

46. Virgin Islands Annual Medical and Sanitary Report, 1927. *CO 316/13.* At the time, malaria, yaws, gonorrhea, tuberculosis, and heart disease were common. Medical Report, 1927. *CO 316/13.*

47. Lethem to secretary of state, 1936. *CO 152/465/16.* A nurse from Holberton Hospital in Antigua, Iris Edwards, was appointed matron by the commissioner. Erinita Hodge, a local woman who had worked at the hospital since 1929 and had acted as matron on at least two occasions, was passed over. Medical and Sanitation Report for the BVI, 1936. *CO 316/13.*

CHAPTER 7

The Boom Years, 1970-1995

PROGRESS AND CHANGE

The arrival of greater and greater degrees of self-government in the fifties and sixties brought a heady period of growth and development. Encouraged by the possibility of employment, outward migration tapered off and the population grew. In 1960, the number of males in the Virgin Islands stood at 3,930 and that of females at 3,991. Ten years later the number of males had reached 5,131 and that of females, 4,541.[1] Virgin Islanders were no longer migrating in significant numbers as they once had. The population began to climb. The territory became a draw for immigrants. The trickle that the Community League had hoped to reduce eventually became a flood. According to census 1991 figures, between 1980 and 1991, 2,883 female and 3,058 male immigrants lived in the territory.

The total population in 1991 consisted of approximately 8,263 males and 7,853 females. The Virgin Islands were transformed from what census officials called a "net exporter" of persons to "a net importer." The population composition stood at 50.1 percent nationals and 49.9 percent non-nationals.

Whereas in the 1960s, workers were being paid between $6.00 and $12.00 per day, the per capita income had risen to $7,000 in 1986. The high salaries and rapid developmental pace were fueled not only by the burgeoning tourist industry but also by the financial sector. In 1984, the territory passed the International Business Companies Act, and the islands became a leading corporate domicile.

The changes were marked everywhere. In 1967, Peebles Hospital contained sixteen beds and six cots. The staff consisted of three medical doctors, four staff nurses, eight student nurses, three laboratory technicians, and one public health inspector. More than a decade later, the hospital contained fifty beds, and was served by a staff of twelve physicians, forty-five trained nurses, and several other support staff. The public service, which, in the 1960s, consisted of approximately 145 people, ballooned to contain more than a thousand in the early 1990s. The average annual salary for civil servants rose in that time from less than $3,000 to almost $16,000.

In the meantime, the Crude Birth Rate[2] dropped from 35.2 in 1960 to 24.8 in 1980; by 1991, it stood at 18.2.

The composition of the society was changing, with consequences for all. Virgin Islanders had lived in a closed society for more than a hundred years. The forays made by those seeking work in other islands depleted the population, which, if anything, intensified the people's introverted character. The political unrest of the 1940s, the arrival of representative government, and sudden prosperity changed the nature of life in the small islands. Traditional influences and alliances were threatened by these socioeconomic developments.[3]

The political developments of the 1950s led to unprecedented economic growth in the 1960s and 1970s. In turn, the economic advancements of the late 1980s and early 1990s precipitated a demand for constitutional reform. Exposed by large numbers of immigrants to different political systems and influenced moreover by American democratic ideals as propounded on television, Virgin Islanders wanted greater participation in the running of the country.[4] In 1994, a Constitutional Review Commission appointed by the secretary of state for foreign and commonwealth affairs in the previous year recommended the adoption of a "mixed system." Though opposed by the government of the day, the Foreign and Commonwealth Office adopted this recommendation. In 1995, Virgin Islanders went to the polls to select thirteen candidates for the legislature. The exclusion and distance many women felt from politics seemed at an end. Never before that year's election had so many women run for political office. Never before had any woman won.

The achievement of women politicians came against a backdrop of increased economic and educational opportunities for women. These opportunities situated women in leadership positions much as the colonial authorities of the 1940s and 1950s had situated men in positions of influence and power.

By the end of the 1960s, women filled several important public sector positions. In 1967, Emmogene Creque became the first woman on the Public Service Commission,[5] and in 1970, Paula Beabrun served as magistrate and registrar.[6] Enid Scatliffe became chief education officer in 1974. These women and others like them blazed a trail through the developing public/political life of the colony, which made it easier for the women who followed. Their presence ensured that as the economy expanded, it made space for women.

WOMEN IN THE ECONOMY: GAINING GROUND

In 1980, women made up 37.8 percent of the employed population and accounted for almost three-quarters of the unemployed. According to the census, women in the nonlabor force were concentrated in home duties.

Another way of looking at the same figures makes the position clearer. In 1980, 83.72 percent of males were employed, but only 55.87 percent of women were in the labor force. In fact, 40 percent of females were not in the labor force, compared with 12.34 percent of males. The territory at that time was still concentrating on solidifying the gains made in the previous decades. Industry concentrations were therefore highest in the utility sectors, public administration, and private households. The first two industries were markedly male dominated (only .59 percent of females in the labor force were in utilities as opposed to 19.18 percent of males; 9.83 percent of females in the labor force and 12.30 percent of males were in public administration). Almost 50 percent of women in the labor force in 1980 worked in private households (47.02 percent), whereas only 28.72 percent of men were found in that sector.

Between 1980 and 1991, government concentrated its focus on encouraging development in the tourism sector and in nurturing the fledgling financial sector. The economy expanded, and women surged in to fill the empty spaces. The percentage of females not in the labor force dropped from 40.23 percent in 1980 to 32.3 percent in 1991. The hotel and restaurant sector, in particular, absorbed a lot of women. Women almost doubled their participation in that sector, rising from 12 percent in 1980 to 22 percent in 1991. In fact, they increased their participation in most sectors, including public administration, real estate, and finance.

Further, women's involvement in high-skilled occupations grew from 16.2 percent in 1980 to 22 percent in 1991. Women were commanding 41.3 percent of high-skill jobs that year. As the census reports, "women made substantial gains" in the 1980s. But a closer look reveals that those gains were flawed, affecting only a small percentage of women.

Women are mostly concentrated in clerical and service jobs, and they continue to earn less, on average, than men do. According to the census of 1991, 47.73 percent of females were at the low-income level compared with 37.22 percent of males. In addition only 5.55 percent of females were at the high-income level versus 12 percent of males.[7] Interestingly, although 43.28 percent of men with university-level education earned high incomes, only 15.05 percent of females with the same level of education earned as much. Instead, the majority of highly educated women in the BVI earned middle-level incomes. Even males with only a secondary education were more likely to outearn women with university-level education. Women's earning potential and power are stymied by prevailing stereotypes and prejudices that do not allow a woman to receive remuneration at the same rate as a man.[8]

It can also be argued that men tolerated the work of groups such as the Community League and of individuals such as Valerie Thomas because it was unremunerated. Women's waged work in a sense functions as a tax on men's liberalism or progressiveness. The entrance of more and more women into the workforce has exposed men's unwillingness to pay that tax. Women's heightened involvement in the waged labor force did not signal the dismantling of the patriarchal superstructure erected during slavery and maintained since then. On the contrary it made women's second-class status explicit. Legislation and policies that target or specifically mention women have often been paternalistic in nature. For instance, the Labour Code (1975) allows government to make particular regulations for the protection of women and children. Thus the minister of labor can regulate "the maximum hours of employment of women, young persons or children and the times allowed for meals." The minister may also regulate "the cleanliness, . . . overcrowding, ventilation and general sanitary conditions of any workplace or place wherein women, young persons or children are employed." Similarly, the income of a married woman who lives with her husband is automatically taxed as the income of the husband. If a woman does not like this arrangement, she has to make a special application to be taxed separately.

Though women had definitely increased their participation in the labor force, they tended to be underemployed.[9] The 1991 census indicated that 13.6 percent of females worked for fewer than 35 hours per week, compared with 7.5 percent of males. People who work few hours generally make less money than those who work full time: almost 48 percent of females were low-income earners.[10] As Pateman points out, women in "low-status, low-skilled jobs" are precisely those who are not likely to demonstrate high rates of political participation. Struggling to make ends meet, these women have no sense of owning a stake in their government. Their resources are completely invested in the day-to-day struggle to feed and clothe themselves and their children. Consequently they do not perceive themselves as having any investment in the polity; they have not created the polity, nor are they of it. The economy of the territory may rest on them, in turn fueling political advancement, but these women are largely untouched by the gains made.

Ironically, the high visibility of the women who were heading government ministries and departments helped to create the notion that not only had women "arrived," but they were taking over. By 1995 two out of five permanent secretaries (counting the financial secretary) were women—Lorna Smith and Sebulita Christopher—and the attorney general was also a woman, Dancia Penn. Heads of government departments included Chief Information Officer Sandra Ward, Chief Personnel Officer Magdaline Rymer, Comptroller of Customs Kather Smith, and Accountant General Kharid Fraser, among others. The success of exceptional women such as these paved the way for the subsequent achievements of women politicians. It also provided women with role models who had a public identity, one that was not shaped by their marital and/or parental status. Despite income imbalances, the occupational and other opportunities prevalent in the society did change women's view of themselves and their roles. This is evident from statistics given in the following section. For many women, their participation in the waged labor force created demands that changed and lessened the family's role as women's sole source of a viable identity.

WOMEN AND THE FAMILY

"The high cultural value placed on child-bearing and mothering entails an acceptance of economic responsibility for children [and] also explains the need to work."[11] Women in the Virgin Islands have always worked, but as the nature of the economy changed from one based on agriculture to one based on service, the nature of women's work changed also. Women flocked to jobs in the hotel and restaurant service, and in public administration and the financial sector. Now that their work took them farther from home, childbearing became problematical for women. Also the newfound accessibility of both waged employment and higher education created new ideals for women. Between 1980 and 1991, the Total Fertility Rate (TFR) dropped from 3.1 to 2.0. Women who were not in the labor force recorded a TFR of 4.39. Employed women, on the other hand, had a TFR of 2.04. Women with university degrees registered an even lower TFR of 1.35. Their university education, the economy's expansion, and the introduction of birth control gave women a range of life options to choose from.

Only 8.99 percent of children younger than five were attending school in 1980; by 1991 that figure had risen to 21.8 percent. Women were no longer staying at home to care for their children. Instead, they were utilizing the services of the preschool and day-care centers that had sprung up in the previous decade. Thus women's entry into the waged workforce of the new economy forced societal changes. The numerous day cares and preschools that have been established on Tortola in the last couple of decades is proof of that.

In 1980, females headed 25.4 percent of households, but eleven years later that number had risen to 28.7 percent. An explanation for the rise may be found in the increased number of migrants to the territory, many of whom were women, as has been noted previously. Interestingly, two-person households headed by females were more likely to consist of a single mother and child, whereas those identified as headed by males were most likely to include a spouse or partner. Whatever progress women may have made socially and economically, patriarchal assumptions remained in place. Children are thus primarily women's concern, and where a man is present, he is considered to head the household.

As Barriteau charges, ideological relations of gender have remained unaddressed and unchallenged in the Caribbean even as states have made progress on improving the material relations of gender. Women have equal access by law to the vote, health care, education, and so on, thus effecting an improvement in material conditions. Ideological relations that posit women's subordination have not changed, however. This has particular implications for the familial environment. Women are earning bigger and bigger salaries and have greater and greater choices before them, yet their public advancements have not mirrored private advancements. This is most clearly demonstrated in the consideration of violence against women in the home. According to a UNICEF document, women make daily reports of domestic violence to the police, but the government has been slow to interfere or respond, reluctant to meddle in what conventional wisdom holds to be "man/woman business." It was only in 1988 that the Evidence Act was amended to allow a woman to give evidence against her husband in cases of domestic violence. However, neither the police nor any other agency collects accurate data on the incidence of domestic violence in the territory.

Similarly, until very recently, a woman could not charge her husband with rape, and a man could petition the court for the restitution of conjugal rights if the wife was guilty of not cohabiting. Women had no corresponding right to apply for the restitution of conjugal rights.[12]

Ironically, women's dominant parenting role as single heads of household and as wives and mothers is not always supported by legislation. For instance, Section 5 of the Wills Act gives the father but not the mother the power to dispose by will the custody of a child.[13]

The colonial patriarchal legacy has also survived in laws such as Regulation 6 of the Pensions Amendment Regulations (1962), which provides for women's early retirement from the civil service upon marriage. In fact, General Orders, the code of conduct under which civil servants function, still allows women with more than five years of pensionable service to resign from the civil service upon marriage and collect a gratuity. According to Section 8.15(2):

A female officer who has not less than five years pensionable service may, on marriage, exercise the option to resign and take a marriage gratuity under the provisions of the Pensions Regulation. Such option, which will be irrevocable, must be taken within three months of the date of marriage and if the option is not exercised in writing within the specified period it will be deemed that the female officer has elected to continue her pensionable service.[14]

Official philosophy held that women, once married, should be encouraged to quit. Section 8.15(3) makes this even more explicit:

A female officer whose domestic responsibilities interfere with the discharge of her official duties may be called upon to resign, in which case she will be eligible to receive the marriage gratuity for which she would have been eligible at the time of her marriage.[15]

Virgin Islands women, then, were considered to have weakened their claim to public life by marrying. After marriage they became wives with all the duties and responsibilities traditionally associated with wifedom, thereby incapable of handling those obligations that took them outside the home. The home was in fact the sphere to which she was expected to devote all her energies, but by doing that, by fulfilling society's expectations of the wife, her presence in the workplace became suspect. Quite unlike the modern metropolitan woman who, in the sixties and seventies, was staking her right to "having it all," Virgin Islands women were expected to know both their limitations and their "true" priority—the family.

Another law that made clear women's continuing subservient legal position is the British Nationality Act of 1981. Modeled on the British Nationality Act of 1948, this act stipulates who is entitled to BVI citizenship. Under it, only men can confer Belonger status on their foreign-born spouses. Further, any woman who gains Belongership through certification or marriage loses it when she marries a non-Belonger. The constitution of the Virgin Islands also makes these provisions. Under Section 2 (f) a wife shall be "deemed to belong" only if she "is not living apart from" a husband who gained Belongership through certification or if there is no deed of separation between them. Section 2 (h) ii declares that a "woman shall cease to be deemed to belong to the Virgin Islands . . . if she marries a person who is not deemed to belong to the Virgin Islands." The vulnerability of women's national identity is, therefore, significantly greater than that of men. Women's Belongership status depends on men. A divorce or their husband's death and their subsequent remarriage will affect them in ways that men are not affected. Amendments to the Constitution, gazetted on 8 June, as well as the Immigration Bill, not yet presented to the legislature (as of 18 August), will effect sweeping changes expected to improve women's nationality status.

The various laws cited and the General Orders point to women's second-class status and how that status has been influenced and designed by colonial policy. General Orders is a direct import from the mother country, and the provisions of the constitution are influenced by the British Nationality Act. The latter is the foundation of Virgin Islands political society, whereas the former should be the leading guide for professional conduct in the territory. Yet, in both, women are clearly perceived as intruding or poaching on male preserves as both workers and citizens. They are not seen as professionals or citizens in their own right but as appendages of men.

Upon marriage they are expected to retire to their proper private sphere as embodied by the household. If Belongers by marriage, their claims to citizenship become vulnerable upon divorce.

Yet an investigation into women's roles in Virgin Islands society and their presence in law reveals an emerging and deepening divergence between local patriarchal ideology and colonial patriarchal politics. Signs of this can be seen from as far back as the 1930s, when British women were appointed to the Moyne Commission yet no local woman was appointed to meet with the commission. The Colonial Office's decision to override the 1950 proposal by Virgin Islands men to deny the vote to women is another sign of diverging patriarchies. In 1986 the United Kingdom extended the United Nations Convention on the Elimination of All Forms of Discrimination Against Women (CEDAW) to two of its Dependent Territories in the Caribbean, the Virgin Islands and the Turks and Caicos Islands. The convention requires governments to take steps to promote women's socioeconomic advancement while reassessing women's role in the family. According to the first CEDAW report made to the UN Committee on CEDAW through the United Kingdom, the Virgin Islands government amended the Matrimonial Causes Act in 1986 to further compliance with the convention's provisions. Under the act women can now have a domicile independent of their husbands, and husbands can no longer sue a third party for damages on the grounds of adultery (a remedy that was not extended to wives). Clearly, the United Kingdom's international obligations as well as national dynamics have forced changes in the government's response to both the material and ideological relations of gender as they are played out in the United Kingdom and in its relations with the Overseas Territories. But women's rights in the Virgin Islands have not been a major focus of UK policy, which is much more concerned with drug trafficking and the regulation of the financial services sector. Certainly, the history of colonial patriarchal power has been too deeply entrenched in both the colonial psyche and that of the colonized to readily give way or be influenced by movements in the Mother Country.

Understanding the tenuous nature of their presence in the polity, Virgin Islands women, as we have seen, staked out other areas of influence. Seizing on fields ignored by men, such as education and nursing, they laid claim to the society in ways that were not dependent on their political status or presence. In doing so they influenced the development of the territory in potent ways.

WOMEN AND SOCIAL POLICY

Since the 1970s, several new volunteer organizations run by women have been established. Only a few have played an important role in sensitizing the society to issues of special concern to women. The Family Support Network (FSN) is one such organization. Formed in 1989 by Marlene Penn with the help of several other women, the network was initially associated with St. George's Anglican Church in Road Town.[16] It was created to "respond to a growing concern about the extent and severity of family problems and violence in the BVI." The goals of the FSN include preventing and relieving family dysfunction "including, but not limited to, domestic violence." The FSN also hopes to "establish and maintain a multi-purpose crisis counselling centre . . . raise community consciousness concerning the prevalence of social problems including domestic violence . . . provide temporary shelter for critical emergency cases . . . and make referrals to other existing agencies." Its target groups are "persons hurting from abuse (physical, mental, alcohol and/or drug related), young couples, young persons, single parents, persons who may feel overburdened and stressed from raising children and the pressures of everyday life . . . abused children and persons feeling the pain of loneliness."

Though most victims of domestic violence are women and most perpetrators are men, the language FSN uses downplays these irrefutable facts. Again when discussing single parents, the FSN fudges on the issue of gender relations. The network's failure to address the issues from a feminist perspective is unfortunate.[17] In refusing to offer a critique of violence against women and its role in patriarchal society, the FSN fails to address core issues. Instead, the network's tentative language demonstrates and reinforces the fact that "even being interested in and seeking knowledge of women's lives and the different conditions of the sexes can be considered threatening."[18] The fact that the FSN identifies itself as "Christian in its approach" helps to explain its emphasis on the "family." Critiques of the ways in which the concept of family has been used to justify women's subordination to men will not be forthcoming from the organization, but its contributions to women's welfare are important. Aware of it or not, in establishing the shelter, the network offers a not-so-subtle challenge to patriarchal assumptions. Through the shelter and its other programs, the FSN offers women the choice that patriarchy seeks to deny them. Further, by establishing the shelter, the network signaled the seriousness with which it viewed the problem and posed a subliminal challenge to government and other institutions. The shelter is a concrete and public reality testifying to something that has had a very private and, in the absence of statistics and testimony, amorphous existence.

Women's impact on social policy, though they were outside of conventional politics, is most firmly demonstrated in the history of the Women's Desk, an organ of the government designed to promote women's political, social, and economic advancement. In 1988 a national seminar on women identified inadequate child-care services, the abuse of women and children, the lack of representation by women within the legislature, and inadequate legal coverage for women as the most pressing issues facing Virgin

Islands women. Following that seminar the Women's Focal Point, an um-
brella group of several women's organizations, lobbied the Lavity Stoutt
government for the establishment of an office to deal with the issues identified. Taking a pro-active feminist position, the Focal Point proposed that
the government establish a Women's Desk to sensitize government ministries to gender issues in the planning and execution of projects; research,
analyze, and supply information about women in the territory; coordinate
the activities of women's groups; organize and facilitate education programs and projects for improving women's economic welfare; establish relationships with external funding agencies; promote the harmonization of
women's goals within national development; promote a legal framework
to support and promote the welfare of women; promote the full representation and participation of women within the highest decision-making bodies; ensure progress on women, health, and development goals; and
facilitate the implementation of the United Nations Convention on the
Elimination of All Forms of Discrimination Against Women (CEDAW).

   Though subsequent government budgets made provision for the Desk,
it was not staffed until 1992.[19] Its terms of reference do not differ significantly from the proposal outlined by the Focal Point, above. The Desk is ad-
ministratively located within the chief minister's office. Since its
establishment it has been responsible for a range of initiatives, including
the formation of a law reform committee and the establishment of a
Women's Studies section at the public library. A major focus of the Desk
has been the elimination of violence against women. Activities toward
achieving this end have included annual seminars for police officers and
social workers and public education programs. Yet, perhaps more than
anything else, addressing the issue of violence against women strikes at the
heart of ideological relations of gender in which women are considered
subordinate to men. Virgin Islands men have articulated, privately and
publicly, their right to "discipline" their women. Many believe that this is
their right as the head of their household or simply as the superior being.
Many see no connection between the abuse of women in their homes and
women's status in society. As Barriteau suggests, governments' failure to
address ideological relations of gender affects their efforts to remedy material relations of gender. One case of violence dealt with by the Women's
Desk involved a woman who wanted to earn a certificate at the local college. Her husband threatened to beat her if she signed up to take classes.
She did, and he made good on his threat. Another case involved a woman
who had been married for several years but decided after her children were
grown that she wanted to work and earn her own money. (Her husband, as
the sole breadwinner, controlled all her finances.) She did not tell her husband her plan, but after the first day of work, he assaulted her, threatening
to beat her every day that she went to work. She never returned to her job.
The state's refusal to effectively challenge women's inequality in the home

ably sabotages women's ability to participate as equals with men outside the home and in the workplace, the school, or the legislature.

The establishment of the Desk was a victory for women's groups. It convincingly demonstrated how women, in their alliances with each other, could shape and form governmental policy. The Desk's location within the chief minister's office with access to the Government Information Service is essential to its high profile. Unfortunately, it has not achieved many of the desired goals.

The most significant problem facing the Desk is staffing. With only one person at the office, it has been seriously hampered in its aims and objectives. Link with other ministries and departments are not of a structured nature but rest more on personal relationships. Women in rural areas are not being as well served by the Desk's evening programs as women in Road Town. The sister islands are almost completely neglected. Government's failure to properly supply the Women's Desk with staff and an adequate budget begs the question of its support. The fact that the recommendations of the Law Reform Committee created at the behest of the Desk never made it past the Executive Council is revealing. The proposals required sweeping changes to criminal and civil legislation affecting women. Suggested among the recommendations were stiff penalties for rape and indecent assault and amendments to the constitution and other acts that would have eliminated their discriminatory provisions. The failure to act on the committee's recommendations suggests that the Desk is not to succeed in making any lasting, institutionalized threats to patriarchal authority.[20]

Another women's group founded in the 1980s is the Tortola Ladies Club (TLC), which was established in 1981. It has a significant expatriate composition and provides grants and services to special projects such as the Council on Alcohol and Drug Abuse and the Adina Donovan Home for the Elderly. The club also sponsors an annual scholarship to the H. Lavity Stoutt Community College. The club holds frequent fund-raisers and sponsors talks for members on various topics, including breast cancer and domestic violence.

The TLC has not adopted a political stance. It is in fact a traditional or conventional women's organization following moderate social welfare objectives. The TLC's composition of mainly British and American expatriates may be a factor in preventing the development of a focus on serious social concerns about the status of women.

Other women's organizations in the territory include the Methodist Women's Guild and the Lions Club of Tortola II. These organizations are composed primarily of Virgin Islands women, but they too confine themselves to traditional women's interests—their focus being welfare work that is not necessarily targeted at women. Like the TLC, the clubs concentrate their welfare work on the Adina Donovan Home for the Elderly, Peebles

Hospital, and other such gender neutral institutions. Although the TLC might prefer, given its membership, to exclude itself from any activity or work that might even be remotely political, the possible reasons for the guild's and the Lions Club's aloofness lie in different areas. As a church organization, the guild may find it difficult to involve itself in controversial issues such as domestic violence and the status of domestic workers. Age brings conservatism to institutions, and although the Methodist Church may once have acted to subvert the status quo in relation to the slaves, it has been the church of choice for the majority of generations of Virgin Islanders.

Meanwhile, the Lions Club is an international service organization whose policies prohibit local chapters' participation in politics. This may explain the local club's reluctance to involve itself in women's issues.

More importantly, the women drawn to join organizations such as the guild and the Lions Club will be those who are not particularly interested in social reform. The organizations attract women who are interested in providing assistance to disadvantaged individuals, not women who want to address the underlying societal conditions that created many of the disadvantages. It is therefore unlikely that organizations such as these will have much impact on improving the status of women in any broad or generalized way. It could rather be argued that their service work, by buffering the impact of government policies, quells dissatisfaction before it can be translated into rebellious action. These organizations then, composed almost solely of women in the middle and upper classes, are involved and invested in the status quo. In this they are no more than a reflection of their society.[21]

Groups such as the Home Industries Committee, which served rural women in the 1930s, and the Family Support Network, which provides services to women in crisis, have served to remind the government of conditions affecting the disadvantaged in the society. These organizations' very existence serves as a rebuke to governmental policies that focus on economic development to the detriment of social development. But because economic development has been given priority over other forms, women's contributions have not been acknowledged. Women's mobilization has not focused on public demonstrations, party organization, and political candidacy, so it is not recognized as having influenced the polity. Yet many of the territory's leaders are products of women-run schools. Women's service as midwives and healers, and as teachers and community workers, has provided the balance lacking in governmental programs geared at effecting the territory's economic advancement.

NOTES

1. Raymond Phillips, 1980–1991 Population and Housing Census of the Commonwealth Caribbean: National Census Report, British Virgin Islands (Guyana: CARICOM, 1991), p. 6.
2. Measured as births per thousand.

3. According to the census, Anglicans and Methodists accounted for 66.5 percent of the population in 1980; by 1991, their share had fallen to 49.6 percent. Other sects, some of which are closely associated with Christian fundamentalism, had increased their shares. So too had both the Hindu and Muslim religions. Phillips, p. 38.

4. Of course, the large numbers of immigrants may also have resulted in a growing sense of marginalization that natives might have sought to combat by an increased say in government.

5. Women's Desk, Office of the Chief Minister, *Women in the Legislative Council* (Tortola: Government of the Virgin Islands, 1997), p. 9. The commission makes recommendations on the management and staffing of the civil service.

6. Ibid., p. 4. Though Beaubrun was a Grenadian expatriate hired on contract, her appointment was nevertheless important because, in 1973, she became the territory's first female attorney general. As such, she was a member of both the Executive and Legislative councils. In 1992, Dancia Penn became the first native attorney general.

7. Phillips, p. 172. Low income is defined as $500 or less per month.

8. The census revealed that 38.66 percent of male managers earned high incomes, as opposed to 21.29 percent of female managers. Additionally, males outearned women in every one of the lucrative sectors such as transportation and communications, and financial and real estate. Phillips, p. 172.

9. Underemployment is usually defined as work that employs short hours, is low income, and is marked by underutilization of skills and low productivity. People considered as underemployed must be dissatisfied with those conditions and express a desire to change them. Phillips, p. 124.

10. Thirty-seven percent of males were low-income earners. Phillips, p. 126.

11. Pauline van der Aa. *Changing Power and Autonomy of the Caribbean Woman* (Santiago, Chile: Women and Development Unit, Economic Commission for Latin America and the Caribbean, 1995), p. 30.

12. The Criminal Code of 1997 now allows a woman to charge her spouse with rape, but only if there is a separation agreement between the couple or she has taken out a restraining order against him.

13. Banks-Denovish and Flemming-Banks, p. 26.

14. General Orders for the Public Service of the British Virgin Islands (1971), revised in 1982 (Government of the British Virgin Islands), p. 43.

15. Ibid.

16. The network now operates under the auspices of the BVI Christian Council, which includes the Anglican, Methodist, and Roman Catholic churches and the Church of God of Prophecy.

17. Carillo quotes a 1987 Report for the Commonwealth Secretariat, which stated that "the abuse of women can be seen as the naked display of male power, the outcome of social relations in which women are kept in a position of inferiority to men." Roxanna Carillo, "Violence against Women: An Obstacle to Development" in *Women's Lives and Public Policy: The International Experience,* ed. Meredith Turshen and Briavel Holcomb (Westport, CT: Greenwood Press, 1993), pp. 99–114.

18. Anna G. Jonasdottir, "On the Concept of Interest, Women's Interests and the Limitations of Interest Theory" in *The Political Interests of Gender: Developing*

Theory and Research with a Feminist Face, vol. 20, ed. Kathleen B. Jones and Anna G. Jonasdottir (London: Sage Publications, 1988) p. 43.

19. The earliest Women's Desk in the Caribbean was founded in Jamaica in 1974. Since then national machineries for women have been established in Grenada and Dominica (1979), Guyana (1980), Belize (1981), Barbados (1984), and most of the other English-speaking Caribbean islands.

20. A Domestic Violence Act passed in 1996 makes it easier for women to get restraining orders against their abusers.

21. Though the earlier Community League was also composed of elite women, the 1960s and 1970s were a time of political, social, and economic turbulence. At that time Virgin Islanders, recently politicized, were very much involved in trying to determine the future of the territory. The society's effort of later decades has mostly been given over to consolidation and expansion of the political and economic gains made previously.

CHAPTER 8

Political Women

POLITICAL GAINS SINCE 1970

In 1971, Millicent Mercer became the first woman to run for office in the Virgin Islands. As a member of the fledgling Virgin Islands Party, Mercer ran in District Five against the leader of the United Party, Conrad Maduro, and Democratic Party hopeful Henry Hodge.[1] Mercer was a primary-school teacher and mother of thirteen who had made her living from handcrafts when she took a leave of absence from teaching. "I decided to try because I agree that women must become involved for the good of all," Mercer said, explaining her decision to run. She clearly saw herself as a trailblazer. "I feel that by stepping forward, it will encourage other women to show the necessary interest in the affairs of the Territory. Men are not the only ones to lead and to work for progress; women must also do their part."[2]

Viewed at a distance, her candidacy seemed destined for failure. She was a novice running against the veteran of at least one previous political campaign who was also the leader of his party. The fact that the VIP was new and untested, a breakaway from the United Party, might have led many to question its legitimacy and chances for longevity and stability.[3] Further, traditional employment stereotyping was then very much in effect, and ideas on gender roles were much more entrenched. The United Party leader won the seat, and more than a decade passed before women ran again.

In the meantime, in 1973, the Constitutional Commission comprising Sir
Colville Deverell and Harvey Lloyd da Costa recommended the introduction of a partial at-large system in which some representatives would be
elected by their district and some by the territory as a whole. Some of the
Deverell/da Costa recommendations were implemented in 1977 when the
number of electoral districts was raised from seven to nine and the voting
age was lowered to eighteen. But the Wheatley government of the day opposed the introduction of the at-large system, as did its successors.

In 1983, Patsy Lake and Eileene Parsons ran for office. Lake ran with the
VIP, whereas Parsons ran as an independent. Parsons contested the District
Five seat but was defeated by political veteran Cyril Romney, who went on
to head the government. Lake also was unsuccessful.

Three years later three women ran for the Legislative Council. They were
Malcia Hodge, who ran on the VIP ticket in District Two; Eileene Parsons,
who ran as an independent in District Five; and Patsy Lake, who ran on the
VIP ticket, also in District Five. The significance to Virgin Islands women of
the nursing and teaching professions has already been discussed, so it is important to note that Hodge was a former nurse and Parsons, a former
teacher. Lake, a cofounder of the People's Action Movement of the 1960s,
was then a businesswoman with a background in cosmetology.

In her newspaper advertisements, Hodge focused on education, the
construction of community centers, illegal drugs, and the encouragement
of culture. Putting an end to drug trafficking was also a major issue with
Lake. Illegal drugs were on the agenda of most politicians as the territory's
increasing use as a transhipment point for cocaine and marijuana bound
for the United States was making headlines within the territory.

Parsons ran on a platform that promised to return honesty to the country. "Vote for men and women who are honest, who will guide the country
with morality and decency while still striving to bring some measure of
prosperity and better living conditions for all the people," she said in one
advertisement.[4] Parsons clearly was going on the offensive against the incumbent. In that year a scandal had broken over the alleged involvement of
the District Five incumbent (who was also the chief minister) in a
money-laundering operation. The governor, exercising his reserve powers,
dissolved the legislature on 21 August 1986, heading off the no-confidence
vote that was scheduled to be called in the House. Elections (which were
not constitutionally due for another year) were scheduled for slightly more
than a month away on 30 September. The voter's list of 1983 was used.[5]
None of the women was elected.

In 1990, two newcomers—former educators Medita Wheatley and Inez
Turnbull—joined the three women who ran in 1980. Both were independents. The former promised to improve education, create a balance between
social and economic development, and ensure the Legislative Council's
consultation with the people if elected. Turnbull's campaign emphasized

the need for better health and medical programs, better housing, improved education, programs for youth, and improvements to the agricultural and fishing industries. The identification of these "people issues" clearly demonstrated women's concern that any type of development should benefit the population and lead to an improved standard of living for all. Coming from behind, women understood well the connection between poverty and powerlessness.

But the difficulty of unseating an incumbent was demonstrated once again at the polls: all were returned to office. The unshakeable grip these men held on their district seats seemed to prove the need for constitutional changes. But it was the decision of the United Kingdom to abolish capital punishment in its dependent territories that acted as the catalyst for change.[6] Government ministers petitioned the Foreign and Commonwealth Office (FCO) for a review of the constitution. Their aim was to seek greater autonomy along the lines enjoyed by Bermuda, which was exempted from the Order in Council removing the death penalty.

Consequently, a Constitutional Review Commission was appointed in 1993 and submitted its recommendations to the FCO the following year. When the report was forwarded to the Virgin Islands, it was accompanied by a brief announcement. "I have accepted the commission's recommendation that provisions for additional members of the Legislative Council should be introduced in time for the next dissolution and general election," wrote Douglas Hurd, then secretary of state for foreign and commonwealth affairs.

Within the system recommended by the commission, voters would have a chance to choose both a district and a territorial representative. Four additional representatives elected at large would join the nine district representatives currently sitting in the legislature. The commissioners noted that the change was desired by many of the people who attended their public meetings and made submissions. "Any analysis of the . . . evidence [the Commissioners] received would show that [the mixed system] was nationally regarded as a most important mechanism for bringing some balance and equity to democratic government in the BVI . . . those members elected at large will bring to bear a wider spectrum of ideas on parliamentary debates, better representing the diverse views of the populace and demonstrating a greater commitment to the national interest."[7]

The commission's recommendation and the speed with which it was adopted drew fire from the chief minister. "The action is rather insulting as it presupposes that it does not matter what the majority of the people of the BVI think," the chief minister said in an interview. Apparently fearing a marked loss of control at the polls, a delegation of government officials was quickly put together. Despite indications from the United Kingdom that the change was "non-negotiable" the delegation flew to London to petition either for an outright abrogation or at least for a delay in implementation. Their efforts were in vain.

Of the six women who ran for office in March 1995, five offered themselves as at-large or territorial candidates. The decision of the majority of the women candidates to run at large suggests a prioritization of national over district interests. Certainly the fact that five of the women came out of a strong background in cultural, welfare, or church work that was not restricted to the district in which they lived must have affected their decision. Lake was the president of the BVI Horse Racing Association, a member of the Tortola Ladies Club, and a founding member of the Lioness Club (now the Lions Club II). Turnbull was cofounder and director of the Methodist Church Young People's Choir, secretary for the BVI Christian Council, and deputy director of the BVI Red Cross. Parsons was the founder of the BVI Heritage Dancers, a former chairperson of the BVI Festival Committee, secretary general of the BVI Olympic Committee, and a member of the Tortola Ladies Club. Women's involvement in these organizations and their history of islandwide community work lifted them above the parochial interests required of district candidates. It also made them known outside of the communities in which they lived.

The fact that almost all of the women chose to run at large points to their understanding of the limits of the district system, which favors the incumbent. It also shows their awareness of the need for a convincing win. None of them would have been blind to the fact that winning a territorial seat would have been a conclusive and convincing response to questions raised about women's lack of political acumen and their fitness for political roles.

Interestingly, all six women candidates, in both the at-large and the district race, ran as independents. Only two of them won their respective races. Veteran campaigner Eileene Parsons was the top vote-getter of the at-large candidates, and another, newcomer Ethlyn Smith, succeeded in unseating the District Five incumbent of more than ten years.[8]

At least one observer saw the women's win as a sign that "the territory is maturing politically." "With the last few remaining years in this century, BVI voters have signalled their readiness at last for a change from the male bastion that had previously characterised the legislature. That's progress," *The BVI Beacon* editorialized.

FACTORS AFFECTING WOMEN'S POLITICAL PARTICIPATION

The success of women at the polls in 1995 was the eventual end of a special and particular concatenation of events that began with women's community work during and after slavery. Koven says of European women's volunteer associations that they were "sites for the expression and growth of women's civic and political consciousness." The same is undoubtedly true for women in the Virgin Islands, but until the developments of the 1960s and 1970s, the difficulties of travel impeded women's contact with women outside their community. That factor combined with the territory's political stagnation at the time acted to retard the development of women's consciousness and also to localize their work within the community.

The territory's economic development in the 1970s propelled infrastructural changes. The creation of a fairly extensive road system on Tortola allowed for ease of travel within the island. Women now found it easier to form associations and links that were not necessarily family or community based but were islandwide and demonstrated a broader interest base.[9] Though they continued to be absent from conventional politics, women, either individually or through their associations, contributed significantly to policy formation. It was their activism that led to the creation of governmental machinery to address the issues and problems affecting women that in turn influenced some legislative reform. Women were increasingly aware of the need to be collectively present as women within the political arena, and they accomplished this through their volunteer associations. This created an environment in which women's eventual political emergence was inevitable.

Their entrance into the waged labor force had an even deeper impact. Theorists suggest that women's unequal earning power relative to men produces or gives rise to gender politicization. Women in the Virgin Islands certainly made strides in the 1980s and 1990s. More and more of them were heading government departments, earning university degrees, and holding senior positions in the private sector. But their salaries were not keeping pace with men's. Not only were men making two and three times what women made, they were outearning women with more education. If women had previously believed that their failure to gain office or to hold certain key positions was related not to a hostile "social arrangement" but to personal failings, their increased participation in the waged labor force awakened them to material patriarchal realities that challenged this belief. Some women may therefore have experienced a rise in gender politicization upon recognizing the inequalities of the workplace. Their awareness of the need for women to act collectively may have led to women's victories at the polls in 1995.

If the success of women politicians does not, however, translate into material improvements in the lives of the masses of women who continue to hold low-level jobs and/or are underpaid, women's politicization may seem irrelevant to women themselves. Further, the ability of less than a handful of elected women to influence the polity is doubtful. It depends on their numbers and on their willingness to forge an alliance. At least two more women need to join their female colleagues in the legislature if the critical mass needed by a minority to affect the dominant culture is taken to be 30 to 35 percent.

Women's success was also encouraged by a contradiction. The British government had exercised its powers to remove the death penalty.[10] In response, the local government demanded a constitutional review through which it hoped to expand its powers and exercise a greater degree of sovereignty. Ironically, this tactic backfired when Britain issued an ultimatum to change the Elections Act or else have it done in the United Kingdom. The system immediately forced change within the parties, which had to open their doors to newcomers if they wanted to offer a full slate of candidates.

By 1980, the two main parties in the territory were the United Party (UP) and the Virgin Islands Party (VIP), which had splintered from the UP in 1971.[11] The VIP, headed by H. Lavity Stoutt, who had himself never lost an election since 1957, was widely regarded as the dominant party.[12] It was in control of the government five times between the inception of ministerial government in 1967 and the elections of 1995.[13]

But political parties in the Virgin Islands have not functioned like parties in other countries. They have not held conventions or had membership systems. It has been said that they are "necessary to an event—the general election but not as part of the ongoing political process." One critic charged that "in truth and in fact, we don't have political parties. We have men who get together and get in the Legislature." Colonial officials co-opted or hand-picked the people's leaders or so-called representatives. Thus co-option became a legacy of the colonial system. Local political leaders subsequently used co-option to draft other men into politics. As partners and associates in such bastions of power and influence as the Rotary Club of Tortola, men make and solidify their associations with each other, often in the absence of women.

Women are excluded from these cliques. Even in those instances when women made their way onto a party's slate, the masculine culture they encountered there undermined any possible advancement. Women's eventual success at the polls may, in fact, have depended heavily on their rejection of the parties.

Certainly, the slate of candidates offered by the major parties changed little over the years. Indeed, there was little need to do so in a system that rewarded the incumbent who kept his district happy. As has been noted, the leader of the Virgin Islands Party won every election from 1957 until his death in 1995. Though he was the most long serving of politicians, he was by no means the only one to have served multiple terms. One former chief minister represented District Five for fourteen years. A politician from District Three lost only one election between 1971 and 1995. Most have served at least two terms.

The dominance of the VIP makes it the party of choice for many hopefuls, but its failure to support its women candidates means that many women have a love/hate relationship with the party.

In 1986, Eileene Parsons, running as an independent, urged voters to "forget the parties," but in 1990, she ran as a VIP candidate. In 1986, Patsy Lake, a VIP hopeful, wrote that "independent candidates . . . have become extinct in the rest of the world and we must now do the same if we are to develop and be respected." But Lake ran as an independent in the 1995 elections, as did Parsons.

In 1986, the VIP fielded two women candidates (Malcia Hodge of District Two and Patsy Lake of Dictrict Five) out of a slate of nine, but it did not do so again until more than a decade later, in 1999. Only one other party, the Progressive People's Democratic Party in 1990 (Malcia Hodge of Dictrict Two) had ever fielded a woman candidate prior to the 1995 elections.[14]

Interestingly, none of the sister islands has ever produced a woman candidate, a situation that might be explained by the effect of the district system. Virgin Gorda, the second-largest population center of the Virgin Islands with 2,437 people, is, along with Anegada, part of District Nine.[15] The District Nine representative, a member of the VIP, has been in office since 1975. Jost Van Dyke, the third major population area (population 140) falls within District One, which had been represented by Lavity Stoutt of the VIP since 1957. The isolation of sister islands such as Anegada and Jost Van Dyke along with their small populations limit the chances that a successful candidate, particularly for the territorial race, will come from those islands. For them the support of a strong party would be crucial.

The obstacles the parties pose to women's participation as political decision makers have not gone unnoticed. An editorial in the *Island Sun* charged that

Their speeches and manifestos notwithstanding, the fact is that parties . . . have not made room for women nor have women brought sufficient pressure to make them do so . . . Women have been accepted as historical heroines but not as real people with an adequate technical background and sufficient political judgement to take part in decision-making and share in the power exercised in the world of day-to-day politics.[16]

Virgin Islanders have given researchers various reasons for the absence of elected females. They include that "politics is too rough a game for women," "women are not interested," and "they are not well prepared." Because women were absent from the leadership of explicitly political groups such as the Civic League and, later on, from the legislature, it was assumed that they were disinterested in politics. Their absence from "the rough game" thus appeared to suggest their frailty and weakness, thereby confirming the rightness and inevitability of their exclusion.

The truth is that the odds of an incumbent regaining his seat are very high, whereas the chances of any newcomer (man or woman, but particularly woman) are nearly nonexistent. It was for these very reasons that the mixed system (territorial and district elections) was recommended. The Constitutional Commissioners of 1973 in encouraging the adoption of the mixed system said, "we feel that it is important to encourage public-spirited persons to offer themselves for election, who because of the essentially parochial nature of the present constitutional system might have little hope of election." It seems they were right about the effect the mixed system could have in galvanizing political participation. Women took five of the top fifteen positions (in a field of twenty-four) in the at-large elections, with two of them beating more seasoned campaigners.

Women's previous exclusion from office also worked in their favor in 1995. Voters declared themselves fed up with what one observer called the "dog-eat-dog scenario." Ending government corruption and alleged nepotism were identified as key issues during the time leading up to the elections. Women were therefore perceived as fresh and uncorrupted outsiders/newcomers. This proved a significant advantage to them.

Further, many voters expressed dissatisfaction with government spending on major development projects such as the cruise ship dock and the Central Administration Building. The women candidates, on the other hand, tended to emphasize social issues such as establishing youth programs and improving the quality of health care and education. "The BVI has enough buildings, roads and retaining walls. Now let us have a government that will concentrate on the development of the people," said at-large candidate Medita Wheatley.

For both male and female politicians, membership in the Methodist Church appears to be a significant factor, as it is a common denominator. At least three of the territory's four chief ministers have been active members of the Methodist Church, serving as society stewards, local preachers, and in other positions.[17] Women can certainly trace their involvement in the Methodist Church from its inception in the 1700s straight through to the present, as previous chapters have demonstrated. In recent times their activism in the denomination with the highest membership in the territory has exposed them to the electorate in leadership positions. In addition, their leadership has placed them in positions where they have learned to hone their organizational, management, and people skills to a fine degree.

But church wasn't the only place where women learned about organizing and from which they drew strength. The education profession has been particularly significant for women politicos. Of the six women who ran for office in 1995, four were former teachers, one was a former civil servant, and another was a businesswoman. As has been noted before, teaching exposed women to overseas training and allowed for their participation in regional education conferences such as the Standing Conference on Teacher Training in the Eastern Caribbean.[18] Women teachers therefore participated in and chaired important meetings with established protocols. By doing so they not only enhanced their considerable organizational abilities

as teachers but also gained a working knowledge of the intricacies of effective leadership. It should also be remembered that until the 1970s, teaching
was one of the few professions open to blacks in the territory. The economy
prior to those years simply did not support many professions. Women
teachers were thus among the few professionals in the territory and were
highly respected as such in their communities.

In considering the participation of women in Virgin Islands politics, it is
also necessary to consider the individual women who have run for office
and the role they play in the private sphere.

With perhaps one exception, the women who ran for office in 1995 were
all over fifty years old.[19] Their age may point to the longer road women
have to travel to achieve financial security and comfort. As has been
pointed out, men in the territory make more money on average than
women do; they have, therefore, more disposable income to devote to a political campaign. Women may have to wait longer to achieve the financial
stability and security needed to invest in a run for political office.

Both of the successful women candidates are unmarried, and one is
childless. Although the numbers are too small to draw conclusions from,
the above facts might suggest that the demands of family have a negative
effect on women's chances for electoral success, perhaps by limiting the
time and finances they can contribute to campaigns. This brings us back to
the age factor. Perhaps it is only after raising children and putting in their
domestic time that women feel they have gained enough credit to pursue
their own concerns. This generation of women was restrained in young
adulthood by the demands of motherhood and what Pateman calls the
"daily routines" of the family. They would have had no time then to com-
mit to the demands of a political career. Thus the absence of younger
women from the field of conventional politics suggests that though women
are juggling home and career, they find it impossible to add political involvement to that list. This suggests women's compliance with the convic-
tion that women's priorities should be with family. Only when they are
past childbearing age do they gain not only the freedom but the social ap-
proval necessary to launch public careers. If they are no longer of childbearing age, they are no longer perceived as sexual beings whose demands
elsewhere might have a negative effect on their performance as representatives of the people. Patriarchal thought limits women to the sum of their reproductive parts, thus determining that women's importance to society
lies primarily in their successful performance as wives and mothers. The
age of the women candidates therefore conferred on them an asexuality
that enhanced rather than diminished their status.

It can be argued then that the particular achievements of certain women
have not transformed the patriarchal underpinnings of the colonial, oligar-
chical society found in the Virgin Islands. The constitutional developments
of the 1950s and the subsequent evolution of government are colluding

with the current party system to deny the masses, but particularly women, a political presence.

The success of exceptional women has not acted as an effective challenge to patriarchy and will not contribute to its eradication or downfall. None of the women candidates has addressed issues relating to the patriarchal and colonial superstructure of the society. Yet gender asymmetry and class hierarchy are interwoven with colonialism. Unless women of all classes mount an explicit and coherent challenge both to colonial power and to patriarchy, they will remain unequal and disadvantaged participants of the colonial state.

As a colony the Virgin Islands is itself in an unequal and disadvantaged relationship with the United Kingdom. Women's location within the pyramid of ultimate power as wielded by Britain is at the very bottom. The "talented tenth" of women may move forward, but they will do it on patriarchal and colonialist terms, and they will leave the majority of Virgin Islands women behind.

Though their campaigns were, in themselves, subversive to patriarchal conventions, the positions some women candidates took underscored those norms. Women did not shy away from proclaiming their identities as women and therefore as being able to bring fresh qualities of leadership to the society. In taking this approach, however, they did not offer any new vision of women's role in society. "I will ensure that the [Legislative] Council becomes sensitive to the needs of women so that they will receive the support that they need in performing the vital role of keeping families together and strengthening the social structure of the territory," said Medita Wheatley.[20] "When our women, the bonding agents of our home structure, are physically broken mentally broken, morally broken, the backbone of our society is broken," lamented Malcia Hodge, the Progressive Peoples Democratic Party candidate for District Two in 1990. To some extent, then, women saw their election to the House as being primarily of benefit to women in the home. The perception of women's special connection to the home and family interests as well as their background in education led many candidates to emphasize issues such as the provision of day care and preschool facilities.

It may well be that identifying with women's traditional interests backfired on the women candidates who used this tactic. The successful women candidates did not closely ally their campaign issues with women's role in the family. In her campaign Parsons stressed the "creation of job possibilities for housewives" and the importance of having "a diversified voice and a say for women of the territory." Ethlyn Smith, on the other hand, took a gender neutral stance on a platform that included tax review, public sector reform, a new land management policy, the enactment of ethics legislation, and a Bill of Rights. In identifying these as issues on which to build their campaigns, these women transcended gender stereotypes. They brought an awareness that women's roles had changed and that they too were in-vested in broader economic, social, and political issues. This was both posi-tive and negative—positive because it showed women candidates in a new light, competing with the boys on the boys' turf; negative because women's concerns were not addressed. Issues such as domestic violence that are not allied with conventional expectations of women's interests but with an awareness of the impact of patriarchal ideology on women's opportunities and lives in the territory received no attention.

Although hailed as a sign of progress, the elections of 1995 revealed just how negligible women's impact continues to be on the political process.[21] The elections saw the highest number of women ever to run for office, but a total of thirty-eight candidates were in the field. Women constituted less than a quarter of those running for office. Social issues received arguably more attention than they had in previous years, but women's issues did not. Of all the party manifestos released in 1995, only one, that of the Virgin Islands Party (VIP), allocated any space to women's issues. In a special sec-tion of the revised edition of the manifesto it first issued that year, the VIP promised to introduce polices to alleviate and prevent sexual harassment and domestic violence, to review employment policies to ensure women equal compensation, and to improve women's status under the constitu-tion. The VIP obviously recognized, at least on paper, that women's roles had changed and that they had special concerns.

The Concerned Citizens Movement said that it was putting "people first," but its platform indicated that the party was concentrating on eco-nomic issues, governmental reform, and youth. Nowhere in its manifesto did it mention women as a special interest group, and it did not offer a sin-gle woman candidate on its slate. The same is true of the United Party.

Clearly, the record number of women running for office that year had lit-tle effect on introducing gender issues into the political discourse. That the successful women candidates themselves did not articulate a position on gender issues or reveal any desire for women's political empowerment suggests that they do not see themselves acting as women's representa-tives. They offer women no feminist vision, because women themselves have not organized around gender issues and can offer them no support. In the absence of a show of gender solidarity, women politicians play it safe by playing to the whole house.

Neither can women afford to completely ignore the parties. The role of the party, particularly when it is the VIP, is significant. In the at-large elec-tion, the leader of the United Party got the second-highest number of votes, but two VIP members followed him. In fact, of the top seven vote-getters, four were VIP who swept the traditional VIP strongholds of Districts One, Seven, Eight, and Nine.

But the fact that none of the women ran with a party and that no woman who did run on a party slate had ever won (prior to 1999) points to deficien-

cies in the party system.[22] The task of supporting women in any space created proves unequal to the tradition of male dominance pervading the
parties (and the society as a whole). Women have been unable to establish a
position in any of the parties, making it doubtful that they can do so when
they join the party in government. Whether the formation of a women's
wing to the various parties would effect any great transformation is doubtful. Feminist Pauline Van de Aa argues that "Autonomy is associated with
collectivity: women must defend the specific interests that they share as
women and must have a voice in determining the direction of development."[23] But Virgin Islands women have not articulated a challenge to the
ideological foundations of their society. Neither have they examined and
recognized how women's lives in the territory prior to and following abolition have subverted those roles. Without these prerequisites women will be
unable to find the power to claim their voice.

Women will also have to fight against the sundering effects of the class
differences that are developing with the increasing sophistication of the
economy. According to the 1991 census, 15 percent of women earned income at or below $500 per month. Although women increased their partici-
pation at most levels of the economy, they continued to predominate at the
low- to middle-income brackets. The existence of income inequalities puts
women at an immediate disadvantage when it comes to their participation
in conventional politics. If women are to achieve equity in representation
and participation, they must raise their voices, as women, to challenge the
patriarchal ideology on which these inequalities have been built.
Achieving collectivity will mean forging lines of solidarity between the talented tenth and the masses of women.

De Beauvoir charges that "the more the male becomes individualised
and lays claim to his individuality, the more certainly he will recognise also
in his companion an individual and a free being."[24] As colonized beings,
however, it is doubtful that Virgin Islands men can come to this recognition. Unable to see themselves as architects of the colonial state, men may
feel a particular attachment to their role as the governors of women. Patriarchal power confers on men an absolute authority over the home that the
colonial power denies them over the territory.

The colonial relationship between Britain and the Virgin Islands continues to change, forming an ambiguous and complicated matrix in which the
party system, fostered by the Westminster model of government, acts to
undermine the development of national identity and to cripple hopes for
independence.

Women, running at large and as independents, have demonstrated their
optimism and faith in national interests. In contrast, the failure of the parties to make space for women, to undertake the political education of the
people, and to evolve into truly representative institutions makes clear
their distrust of mass political involvement. Just as colonialism and patriar-

chy intersect and interact with each other, so do the ideals of equality, fraternity, and liberty. Parties have been afraid and thus unable to address any one of the major Enlightenment ideals, recognizing the threat each poses to the party system as it currently exists. Women stand outside this system. Their apartness can be the source of strength from which their politicization can arise to lead the people to freedom from both colonialism and patriarchy.

NOTES

1. *The Island Sun*, 24 April 1971, p. 6. Since 1963 the District Five seat had been held by Dr. Q. W. Osborne, a "Town Boy" and member of the United Three who went on to form the Democratic Party. Osborne's decision to run in District Four in 1971 left a leadership vacuum in his old district that Maduro, who had lost against him in 1967, was eager to fill.

2. *The Island Sun*, 24 April 1971, p. 6.

3. The VIP was, after all, formed as a result of its leader's refusal to subordinate himself to the United Party's organizational apparatus, however minimal.

4. "Political Advertisement," *The BVI Beacon*, 25 September 1986, p. 8.

5. *The BVI Beacon*, 18 September, 1986, p. 1. The decision to dissolve the legislature and to call for early elections meant that approximately 600 people who had just attained voting age, returned to the island, or been granted Belongership status, were unable to vote. It is difficult to say whether these voters would have turned the tide against the incumbents, most of whom were returned to office. (The District Five representative returned as leader of the opposition.) Young people tend to be less conservative than their elders, and it is possible they could have made a difference if they had voted *en bloc*. The district system would have prevented that, however.

6. At a meeting of the Commonwealth Parliamentary Association in 1991, the Dependent Territories delivered a statement to two British members of Parliament stating that "we are disappointed and even outraged at the manner in which [the abolition of the death penalty] was imposed without proper consultation of the people or their representatives." Elizabeth W. Davies, *The Legal Status of British Dependent Territories* (Cambridge: Cambridge University Press, 1995), p. 331.

7. Rich Blake, "UK Quickly Cleared Way for Four New Seats" *The BVI Beacon*, 2 February 1995, p. 4.

8. Both women served on the Opposition until June 1995, when Ms. Parsons crossed the floor to join the Virgin Islands Party as Minister of Health, Education, and Welfare and Deputy Chief Minister. Both women were reelected in the 1999 elections and Mr. Parsons resumed her previous Ministerial positions. On 20 July 2000 her appointment as Minister was revoked by Governor Frank Savage on the advice of the Chief Minister, Hon. Ralph T. O'Neal. Ms. Smith, who was then on the Opposition, crossed the floor and now acts as Minister of Health and Welfare. Mr. Parsons joined the National Democratic Party and sits on the Opposition with the Party's other five elected members.

9. Of course the difficulties posed by the geography of the Virgin Islands has hampered connections between the women of the different islands.

10. The Caribbean Territories (Abolition of Death Penalty for Murder) Order 1991 was extended to Montserrat, Anguilla, the Virgin Islands, the Cayman Islands, and the Turks and Caicos Islands under the West Indies Act of 1962 by a UK Order in Council. Davies, p. 61. This was not the first time the Virgin Islands had clashed with the colonial authority over the death penalty issue. In 1973 Governor Cudmore commuted a convict's death sentence, sparking demonstrations and a Legislative Council resolution demanding his removal. This was forwarded to the secretary of state and rejected.

11. Other parties such as the Progressive People's Democratic Party and the Independent People's Movement in 1990 have contested elections, but they have not lasted beyond them. Duverger's point that "the simple majority single-ballot system favours the two party system" is well taken. Additionally, because the parties have no end other than the election of members, their death upon failure at the polls is a foregone conclusion. Thus the electoral system colludes with the parties to offer only the facade of democracy. In reality, the people are excluded from the possibility of party membership and therefore from the process of choosing their representatives. The fact that parties do not differ on principles means that voters' only choice is between the "ins" and the "outs."

12. An estrangement between the elected arm of the party, headed by Stoutt, and the party leadership, headed by Conrad Maduro, resulted from Stoutt's refusal to attend party meetings. By the next elections, Stoutt had formed his own party, the VIP.

13. To retain power in 1975, the VIP accepted the former chief minister, then a member of the United Party, as chief minister.

14. These figures are only up until 1995. In 1999, the National Democratic Party fielded one woman candidate, as did the Concerned Citizen's Movement. The latter reflected a move by District Five representative Ethlyn Smith to align herself with a pary.

15. Anegada's population stands at 162.

16. Editorial, *The Island Sun*, 4 August 1990, p. 31.

17. A submission to the Proudfoot Commission in 1966 complained that "we are having local preachers who are professing to be Christians, preaching the word of God and yet running to be elected politicians in every district of the BVI." Though the Methodist Church did offer leadership positions to women as class leaders and Sunday school teachers for instance, women were not allowed to serve as local preachers until the 1990s.

18. Parsons left the Virgin Islands in 1961 to study industrial arts, physical education, and Spanish in New York. Her course was arranged by the Department of Education and the Oswego Award, a training scholarship program given by the State University of New York. *The Tortola Times*, 4 February 1961, n.p.

19. One woman, Ethlyn Smith, had recently retired after thirty-three years in the civil service. "Election '95—The District Candidates" *The BVI Beacon*, 9 February 1995, p. 6. Another woman had been a teacher for nearly 40 years. "Election '95—The At Large Candidates" *The BVI Beacon*, 2 February 1995, p. 6.

20. Wheatley was then campaigning as an independent in District Seven. "Candidate Profiles" *The BVI Beacon*, 8 November 1990, p. 11.

21. Voter statistics are, unfortunately, not disaggregated by sex, so it is impossible to determine what factors influence their vote.

22. The increasing heterogeneity of the Virgin Islands population would lead one to suppose a continuing decline in Methodist membership as opposed to that of other denominations and religions. In this scenario, active Methodist membership may cease to play an important role in shaping political careers, particularly for men. Parties may then become more significant.

23. Pauline van der Aa, *Changing Power and Autonomy of the Caribbean Woman* (Santiago, Chile: Economic Commission for Latin America and the Caribbean, 1995), p. 17.

24. Simone de Beauvoir, *The Second Sex* (New York, 1952; rpt., New York: Vintage Books, 1989), p. 170.

Bibliography

BOOKS AND PAMPHLETS

Abraham, James Johnston. *Lettsom, His Life, Times, Friends and Descendants.* London: William Heinemann Medical Books, 1933.

The Alien Worker and His Family. Conference Proceedings. Charlotte Amalie: College of the Virgin Islands, 1967.

Allsop, Richard. *Dictionary of Caribbean English Usage.* Oxford: Oxford University Press, 1996.

Amadiume, Ifi. *Male Daughters, Female Husbands: Gender and Sex in an African Society.* London: Zed Books, 1987.

Anonymous. *Letters from the Virgin Islands.* London: J. Van Voorst, 1843.

Arnstein, Walter L. *Britain Yesterday and Today: 1830 to the Present.* Vol. 2. Boston, MA: D. C. Heath and Co., 1992.

Banks-Devonish, Linda, and Phyllis Flemming-Banks. *National Report on the Status of Women in the British Virgin Islands.* BVI: Women's Desk, 1994.

Barriteau, Violet Eudine. *Gender and Development Planning in the Post Colonial Caribbean: Female Entrepreneurs and the Barbadian State.* Ph.D. Diss., Howard University, 1994.

Beckles, Hilary Mc.D. *Natural Rebels: A Social History of Enslaved Black Women in Barbados.* London: Zed Books, 1989.

Bell, Wendell, and Ivar Oxaal. *Decisions of Nationhood: Political and Social Development in the British Caribbean.* Denver: University of Denver, 1964.

Blackman, Woodie. *Methodism: 200 Years in the British Virgin Islands.* Bridgetown: BVI Methodist Church, 1989.

British Virgin Island Reports 1955 and 1956, 1959 and 1960, 1970. London: Her Majesty's Stationery Office.

Brontë, Charlotte. *Jane Eyre: An Autobiography.* 1847. Rpt., London: Macdonald Illustrated Classics, 1955.

Bryson, Valerie. *Feminist Political Theory: An Introduction.* New York: Paragon House, 1992.

Burnett, Ermin. "The Bottle Industry." In *Virgin Islands Historical Documents,* vol. 3, no. 1. Tortola: Government of the BVI, 1990.

Burns, Sir Alan. *History of the British West Indies.* 2d ed. London: George Allen and Unwin, 1965.

———. *In Defense of Colonies: British Colonial Territories in International Affairs.* London: George Allen and Unwin, 1957.

Bush, Barbara. *Slave Women in Caribbean Society 1650–1838.* Kingston: Heinemann Publishers (Caribbean), 1990.

Carillo, Roxanna. "Violence against Women: An Obstacle to Development." In *Women's Lives and Public Policy: The International Experience,* ed. Meredith Turshen and Briavel Holcomb. Westport, CT: Greenwood Press, 1993.

Carmichael, Mrs. *Domestic Manners and Social Condition of the White, Coloured and Negro Population in the West Indies.* 1833. Rpt., New York: Negro Universities Press, 1969.

Chaudhuri, Naipur, and Margaret Strobel, eds. *Western Women and Imperialism: Complicity and Resistance.* Bloomington: Indiana University Press, 1992.

Coke, Thomas. *A History of the West Indies Containing the Natural, Civil and Ecclesiastical History of Each Island.* 1811. Rpt., London: Frank Cass and Co., 1971.

College of the Virgin Islands. *The Alien Worker and His Family.* Papers Presented at a Conference Sponsored by the College of the Virgin Islands with the Assistance of a Grant under Title 1 of the Higher Education Act, 1965. USVI: College of the Virgin Islands, 1967.

Coole, Diana H. *Women in Political Theory: From Ancient Misogyny to Contemporary Feminism.* Sussex: Wheatsheaf Books, 1988.

Davies, Elizabeth. *The Legal Status of British Dependent Territories: The West Indies and North Atlantic Region.* Cambridge: Cambridge University Press, 1995.

Dawson, Ivan. *A Brief Outline of a Humble Life.* Tortola: Ivan Dawson, 1993.

de Beauvoir, Simone. *The Second Sex.* 1952. Rpt., New York: Vintage Books, 1989.

Dookhan, Isaac. *A History of the British Virgin Islands, 1672–1970.* Essex: Caribbean Universities Press in association with Bowker Publishing, 1975.

Duverger, Maurice. *Political Parties: Their Organization and Activity in the Modern State.* 1950. Rpt., London: Methuen and Co., 1964.

Eadie, Hazel Ballance. *Lagooned in the Virgin Islands.* London: George Routledge and Sons, 1931.

Early, Eleanor. *Lands of Delight: A Cruise Book to Northern South America and the Caribbean.* Boston: Houghton Mifflin, 1939.

Edwards, Bryan. *The History, Civil and Commercial of the British West Indies, Vol II.* London, 1819. Rpt., New York: A.M.S. Press, 1966.

Eggleston, George T. *Virgin Islands.* Princeton: D. Van Nostrand Co., 1959.

Elshtain, Jean Bethke. *Public Man, Private Woman: Women in Social and Political Thought.* Princeton: Princeton University Press, 1981.

Fanon, Frantz. *The Wretched of the Earth.* France, 1961. Rpt., New York: Grove Press, 1963.
———. *Black Skin, White Masks.* New York: Grove Press, 1967.
Foreign and Commonwealth Office. Records and Historical Services. *Women in Diplomacy, the FCO 1782–1999.*
French, Joan. *Women and Colonial Policy after the 1938 Uprising in Jamaica.* Kingston: University of the West Indies, 1989.
Frett-Georges, Rita, ed. *Challenge and Change: The Awakening of a People. BVI 1967–1992. A Glimpse at the Past and a look towards the Future.* Tortola: Government of the BVI, 1992.
Froude, James Anthony. *The English in the West Indies or the Bow of Ulysses.* London, 1888. Rpt., New York: Negro Universities Press, 1969.
Gordon, Shirley, ed. *Ladies in Limbo: The Fate of Women's Bureaux—Case Studies from the Caribbean.* London: Women and Development Programme, Commonwealth Secretariat, 1984.
Goveia, Elsa V. *Slave Society in the British Leeward Islands at the End of the Eighteenth Century.* Puerto Rico: Institute of Caribbean Studies, University of Puerto Rico, 1965.
Gurney, Joseph John. *A Winter in the West Indies Described in Familiar Letters to Henry Clay of Kentucky.* London: John Murray, 1840.
Hammond, S. A. *Leeward Islands Report on an Enquiry Into the Organization and Salaries of the Civil Service.* London: Her Majesty's Stationery Office, 1952.
Hansen, Emmanuel. *Frantz Fanon: Social and Political Thought.* Dayton: Ohio State University Press, 1977.
Harlow, Vincent, and Frederick Madden. *British Colonial Developments. 1774–1834 Select Documents.* London: Oxford at the Clarendon Press, 1953.
Harrigan, Norwell, and Pearl Varlack. *The Virgin Islands Story.* Essex: Caribbean Universities Press in association with Bowker Publishing, 1975.
———. "The Emergence of a Black Small-Holders Society in the BVI." In *Caribbean Perspectives: The Social Structures of a Region.* New Brunswick: Transaction Publishers, 1991.
Higman, Barry W. "The Slave Populations of the British Caribbean: Some Nineteenth Century Variations." In *Caribbean Slave Society and Economy: A Reader,* ed. Hilary Beckles and Verene Shepherd. Kingston: Ian Randle Publishers, 1991.
History of Guiding in the British Virgin Islands, Diamond Jubilee 1936–1996. Tortola: Caribbean Printing Company, 1996.
Howe, Stephen. *Anticolonialism in British Politics: The Left and the End of Empire 1918–1964.* Oxford: Clarendon Press, 1993.
Jenkins, Charles F. *Tortola: A Quaker Experiment of Long Ago in the Tropics.* London: Devonshire House, 1923.
Jones, Kathleen B., and Anna G. Jonasdottir. *The Political Interest of Gender: Developing Theory and Research with a Feminist Face,* vol. 20. London: Sage Publications, 1988.
Knights, Ian. E. *The BVI: An Outline Guide for Expatriate Contract Employees.* London: The Royal Commonwealth Society, 1977.
Koven, Seth, and Sonya Michel. *Mothers of a New World: Maternalistic Politics and the Origins of Welfare States.* New York: Routledge, 1993.

Leahy, Margaret E. *Development Strategies and the Status of Women: A Comparative Study of the United States, Mexico, the Soviet Union and Cuba.* Boulder, CO: Lynne Rienner Publishers, 1986.

Leeward Islands Census with Tabular Statement and Report. 1891. Rpt., Jamaica: University of the West Indies, Trinidad: Central Statistics Office, 1964.

Lewis, Gordon K. *The Virgin Islands: A Caribbean Lilliput:* Evanston, IL: Northwestern University Press, 1972.

Maurer, William. *Recharting the Caribbean: Land, Law and Citizenship in the British Virgin Islands.* Ann Arbor: University of Michigan Press, 1994.

Miles, Rosalind. *The Women's History of the World.* London: Penguin Group, 1988.

Moskos, Charles C. Jr. *The Sociology of Political Independence: A Study of Nationalist Attitudes among West Indian Leaders.* Cambridge, MA: Schenckman Publishing, 1967.

Murray, Stuart, ed. *Not on Any Map: Essays on Postcoloniality and Cultural Nationalism.* Exeter: University of Exeter Press, 1997.

Parsons, Eileene. *150 Years of Achievement, 1834–1994.* Virgin Islands: Department of Education, 1994.

Pateman, Carole. *The Disorder of Women.* Stanford, CA: Stanford University Press, 1989.

Pateman, Carole, and Elizabeth Gross. *Feminist Challenges: Social and Political Theory.* North Sydney: Allen and Unwin Australia Pty., 1986.

Pateman, Carole, and Mary London Shanley, eds. *Feminist Interpretation and Political Theory.* University Park: Pennsylvania State University Press, 1991.

Patterson, Orlando. *The Sociology of Slavery: An Analysis of the Origins, Development and Structure of Negro Slave Society in Jamaica.* London: 1967. Rpt., Rutherford: Fairleigh Dickinson University Press, 1969.

Penn, Howard. *Memoirs of H. R. Penn: A Personal Account of the History and Politics of the BVI in the 20th Century.* Road Town: n.p., n.d.

Phillips, Raymond. *1980–1991 Population and Housing Census of the Commonwealth Caribbean. National Census Report, British Virgin Islands.* Guyana: Caricom, 1992.

Pickering, Vernon. *A Concise History of the British Virgin Islands: From the Amerindians to 1986.* New York: Falcon Publications International, 1987.

Proudfoot, Mary. *Britain and the United States in the Caribbean.* London: Faber and Faber, 1954.

———. *Report of the Constitutional Commissioner: British Virgin Islands.* London: HMSO, 1965.

Reddock, Rhoda. "Women and the Slave Plantation Economy in the Caribbean." In *Retrieving Women's History: Changing Perceptions of the Role of Women in Politics and Society,* ed. S. Jay Kleinberg. New York: Berg Publishers; Paris: UNESCO Press, 1988.

———. "Women's Organisation in the Caribbean Community from the 19th Century to Today." In *Woman Speak,* no. 26 and 27, December 1990.

Report on the Leeward Islands for the Years 1953 and 1954. London: Her Majesty's Stationery Office, Colonial Office, 1956.

Rodney, Walter. *How Europe Underdeveloped Africa.* 1972. Rpt., Washington, D.C.: Howard University Press, 1982.

Rowbotham, Sheila. *Hidden from History: 300 Years of Women's Oppression and the Fight against It.* 3d ed. London: Pluto Press, 1977.

Ruth, Sheila. "Images of Women in Patriarchy: The Masculinist-Defined Woman." In *Issues in Feminism,* 3d ed., ed. Sheila Ruth. Mountain View, CA: Mayfield Publishing, 1995.

Shepherd, Verene, Bridget Brereton, and Barbara Bailey, eds. *Engendering History: Caribbean Women in Historical Perspective.* Kingston: Ian Randle Publishers, 1995.

Simey, T. S. *Welfare and Planning in the West Indies.* London: Oxford at the Clarendon Press, 1946.

Smith, Anthony D. *Theories of Nationalism.* London: Gerald Duckworth and Co., 1971.

Southey, Thomas. *Chronological History of the West Indies, Vol. III.* 1827. Rpt., London: Frank Cass and Co., 1968.

Spackman, Ann. *Constitutional Developments of the West Indies 1922–1968: A Selection from the Major Documents.* Essex: Caribbean Universities Press in association with Bowker Publishing, 1975.

St. Thomas Aquinas. "Question XCII—The Production of Woman." In *Issues in Feminism,* 3d ed., ed. Sheila Ruth. Mountain View, CA: Mayfield Publishing, 1995.

Strobel, Margaret. *European Women and the Second British Empire.* Bloomington: Indiana University Press, 1991.

Suckling, George. *An Historical Account of the Virgin Islands in the West Indies.* London: Benjamin White, 1780.

Sutton, Constance, and Susan Makiesky-Barrow. "Social Inequality and Sexual Status in Barbados." In *The Black Woman Cross-culturally,* ed. Filomina Chioma Steady. Cambridge, MA: Schenkman Publishing Co., 1981.

Trevor, J. C. *Aspects of Folk Culture in the Virgin Islands.* Ph.D. Diss., University of Michigan, 1950.

Trollope, Joanna. *Britannia's Daughters: Women of the British Empire.* London: Hutchinson and Co., 1983.

Truman, George, John Jackson, and Thomas B. Longstreth. *Narrative of a Visit to the West Indies.* 1844. Rpt., New York: Books for Libraries Press, 1972.

van der Aa, Pauline. *Changing Power and Autonomy of the Caribbean Woman.* Santiago, Chile: Women and Development Unit, Economic Commission for Latin America and the Caribbean, 1995.

Walker, F. Deaville. *The Call of the West Indies.* London: The Cargate Press of the Methodist Missionary Society, n.d.

Waller, John Augustine. *A Voyage in the West Indies.* London: Printed for Sir Richard Phillips & Co., 1820.

Ward-Osborne, Faustina. *Review of Existing Data Bases, Identification of Data Gaps and Development of Gender-Based Indicators: British Virgin Islands.* Tortola: Government of the Virgin Islands, 1995.

Watkins, Frederick Henry. *Handbook of the Leeward Islands.* London: The West India Committee, 1924.

Watson, Richard. *A Defense of the Wesleyan Methodist Missions in the West Indies.* London: Thomas Cordeaux, 1817.

Wentworth, Trelawney. *The West India Sketch Book.* London: Whittaker, 1834.

West India Royal Commission Report. London: HMSO, 1945.

White, Robb. *Our Virgin Island.* London: Victor Gollancz, 1953.

Wieringa, Saskia, ed. *Subversive Women: Women's Movements in Africa, Asia, Latin America and the Caribbean.* London: Zed Books, 1995.

Women's Desk, Office of the Chief Minister. *Women in the Legislative Council.* Tortola: Government of the BVI, 1997.

MANUSCRIPT AND ARCHIVAL SOURCES

Census of 1870. St. Thomas, St. John, and St. Croix.

Leeward Island Census with Tabular Statements and Report, 1891.

West Indies Census of Agriculture, 1961.

Rpt., Jamaica: University of the West Indies, Trinidad; Central Statistics Office, 1964.

Despatches of Government to the Colonial Office. C.O. Public Records Office, London.

House of Commons Parliamentary Papers, 1825–45 and *1888.*

Letters to and from the BVI Community League.

Memorandum from BVI Community League to Commission of Inquiry in the Wickham's Cay and Anegada Agreements, 18 September 1969.

Notes in possession of Linda O'Neal, sister of former BVI Community League President Leona Harney.

Mary Proudfoot. *Report of the Constitutional Commissioner, 1965. British Virgin Islands.* London: HMSO, 1965.

Wesleyan Methodist Missionary Society (London). *West Indies Correspondence General.* 1806–1827.

Letter from Marie O'Neal, 11 December 1997 to author.

NEWSPAPERS AND NEWSLETTERS: 1853, 1949–1995

Tidende
The BVI Beacon
The Island Sun
The Torch
The Tortola Times

Index

About the Author

EUGENIA O'NEAL was Head of the Women's Desk of the Chief Minister's Office for the Government of the British Virgin Islands since its inception in 1982 before taking up her appointment as Deputy Permanent Secretary in the Ministry of Health and Welfare in June 2000.